Become a

Great Reader
and *Writer*
in College

Kay Lopate, Ph.D
University of Miami

Patsy Self Trand, Ph.D
Florida International University

Pinecrest Street Company crest is a trademark of Pinecrest Street Company, Inc. and is registered in the United States.
ISBN-13: 978-1-7323690-1-6
ISBN-10: 1-7323690-1-1

Executive Editor: Carlos Borges
Authors: Kay Lopate and Patsy Self Trand
Book Design and Layout: Alexa Behm
Published independently by Pinecrest Street Company, LLC.
www.pinecreststreetcompany.com
Address 11301 S. Dixie Hwy. Box 566684 Miami FL 33156
Printed in the United States
Contact us at
Patsy Trand, PhD or Kay Lopate, PhD
pinecreststreetco@gmail.com

Selected Books in the Navigating Through College series

Reading, learning, critical thinking, vocabulary, writing skills and testing skills

30 Amazing Reading and Learning Strategies for College Students. (2017) Lopate, Kay and Trand, Patsy Self. Pinecrest Street Company.

Become a great reader and writer in college: Get the basics of reading now. Book 1. (2018). Lopate, Kay and Trand, Patsy Self. Pinecrest Street Company.

Getting the basics of critical thinking for college readers and writers. Book 2. (2019). Lopate, Kay and Trand, Patsy Self. Pinecrest Street Company.

Become an outstanding student in the Historical and Social Sciences. Book 3 (In press). Trand, Patsy Self and Lopate, Kay. Pinecrest Street Company.

Become a remarkable student in STEM. Book 4 (In press). Trand, Patsy Self and Lopate, Kay. Pinecrest Street Company.

Vocabulary university professors say that every college student should know. (2017). Trand, Patsy Self and Lopate, Kay. Pinecrest Street Company.

Making it to graduation: Expert advice from college professors (2nd, ed.) (2018). Lopate, Kay and Trand, Patsy Self. Pinecrest Street Company.

Capturing the experience: My first year in college. (2nd, ed.) (2017) Lopate, Kay and Trand, Patsy Self, Carpenter, Sara, Pinecrest Street Company.

Contact us at
Patsy Trand, Ph.D or Kay Lopate, Ph.D
Pinecreststreetco@gmail.com
Pinecrest Street Company, LLC
11301 S. Dixie Hwy. POBox 566684
Pinecrest, FL 33156

PINECREST STREET COMPANY, LLC.
Pinecrest Street Publishing
www.pinecreststreetcompany.com
Pinecrest Street Company, LLC
11301 S. Dixie Hwy. POBox 566684
Pinecrest, FL 33156

Become a Great Reader and Writer in College: Get the Basics Now

Although technology has dramatically changed the way we communicate, one thing that will never change: the need to be proficient in reading and writing. Our modern society will always need proficient readers to comprehend a variety of literature, text, such as textbooks and legal, scientific technological and medical journals. We also need accomplished writers who are able to communicate this information to us.

Book 1, "Become a Great Reader and Writer in College: Get the Basics Now" is written for college bound students to help ensure they have the reading and writing competency for the more advanced, challenging assignments they will encounter in college.

A key feature that makes this book enjoyable is that instruction has been minimized but the many exercises provide assurance that each skill has been mastered.

"Become a Great Reader and Writer in College" is the first book of the four book series, Taking on the Challenge. Books 2-4 continue with advanced reading and writing skills.

The other books in the series are:

Book 2: **Getting the Basics of Critical Thinking for College Readers and Writers.**

Book 3: **Become an Outstanding Student in the Historical and Social Sciences.**

Book 4: **Become a Remarkable Student in STEM.**

Smart student

Preface to the Student

Congratulations! Taking a college level reading and writing course might be one of the most important decisions you have ever made! We believe, along with other reading experts, that students who are proficient readers and writers have an excellent chance to achieve in practically any college academic area. Why? Because college courses are based on reading, vocabulary, oral and written language.

It doesn't matter what kind of reader or writer you are now. What does matter is that you have enrolled in a reading and writing course and that you want to become a stronger reader and writer!

Have you noticed that people who write well, also read extensively and internalize what they have read to their writing! They are sensitive to writing styles, vocabulary, sentence structure, and language. One characteristic all writers have is that they are continually increasing their knowledge base!

Your goal while pursuing a college degree is to develop a high level of competency in reading and writing. Being able to integrate your own individual thoughts and ideas with what you read will help promote thoughtful, well-crafted compositions. This book, "Become a Great Reader and Writer in College: Get the Basics Now," will help you achieve that goal.

Preface to the Instructor

Reading and writing are acquired skills. Students cannot study the night before and become proficient readers and writers. Students must practice, practice and practice.

Developing competent readers and writers has always been a challenging task for instructors. Until recently, reading and writing classes were taught separately - a writing class and a reading class. The current trend today of teaching reading and writing together as a combined course is a sensible approach.

The expertise of competent writers of expository information is not entirely based on their language and writing ability alone. It is also largely based on the information they have acquired from reading and from their background knowledge and experience.

Our goal in "Become a Great Reader and Writer in College" is to give instructors a text that will advance their student's competency in reading and writing. We want our students to use their broad knowledge base and writing ability to write thoughtful, well-crafted compositions. We believe we have achieved this goal because the instruction and exercises require the student to read, think about what was read, and respond by writing about what was read.

"Become a Great Reader and Writer in College, Book 1" is the first book of the four-part series. Book 1, with its integrated approach to reading and writing, will help provide a strong foundation in reading comprehension, vocabulary, and writing. The many exercises throughout the book are the key to strengthen each chapter's instruction. As students advance in school, textbooks, vocabulary, and writing assignments become more difficult and challenging. We cannot assume that just because a student has consistently scored well in high school, that same student will be able to handle the more challenging assignments in college.

What's Inside

Hook

Each chapter begins with a "hook." The "hook" motivates and arouses interest with a "real life" situation with which students can identify.

Challenges

Each chapter begins with at least one challenge for each chapter that provides an overview of the information that students are expected to learn.

Preview of Chapter

Each chapter begins with an overview of a list of topics that will be discussed.

Instructions

Each chapter has clear, concise instructions supported with examples and useful call outboxes in the margins with "tips" and "reminders."

Passing Standardized Tests

Many students who use this book will need to take a basic skills placement test as an exit procedure for college level courses. This text reviews how to answer exit/basic skills questions that appear on the reading section of the text.

Learning Strategy

Each chapter ends with a learning strategy designed to strengthen reading and writing and to prepare students for their college exams. We recommend that students become familiar with all nine strategies because they will promote learning in current and future classes.

Practice Excercises

Each chapter has reading and writing practice exercises.

Chapter Summary

There is a brief summary at the end of each chapter.

What makes this book so enjoyable to use?

"Become a Great Reader in College: Get the Basics Now" is a book designed to strengthen basic reading and writing skills for all students whether the field of study is higher education, technology, or a vocational area.

• Students enjoy the "concise, to the point" instruction with lots of practice exercises that reinforce the concepts.

• Chapter 3 is titled "The Fun Chapter" because it is entertaining and appeals to all types of readers.

• Chapter 3 has interesting stories about word origins, overused words, proverbs from different cultures, hip-hop expressions, common foreign terms, Shakespearean expressions, new words and phrases, and influences from the Bible.

• The illustrations and artwork complement the instructions and exercises.

• *As we wrote this book, we kept two goals in mind - one was to write a book that students like and want to read and the other was that students would begin to develop a reading and writing habit.*

We believe we have
met our goals!

Table of Contents

1

The Reading and Writing Connection

"You should always have two books…the one you're reading and the one you're writing."

Sterling W. Sill

A short play featuring Jimmy, a high school senior, and his counselor, Mrs. Bennett

Jimmy: I've decided I want to be a newspaper journalist and write about all the crises that are happening all over the world.

Mrs. Bennett: That's a wonderful profession. I assume you know a lot about the different countries, such as their history, leaders, problems, and positions in the world today.

Jimmy: Well, I don't know if I need to know a lot about those things, especially the history part, because I'll writing about what's happening now.

Mrs. Bennett: The problems of the world today are usually the result of history or of what took place before. A newspaper writer needs to be very well read. Tell me, Jimmy, do you like to read?

Jimmy: Reading is OK but I'll be honest with you: I don't read much at all.

Mrs. Bennett: I think you should either find a new profession or develop the reading habit. You'll never be able to write about something intelligently if you don't know anything about its background or context.

Jimmy: OK. OK. I'm interested in Korea. I'll start reading as much about it as I can. Now I remember what you told me a long time ago. You said that people who read are a lot smarter than people who don't read!!!

Mrs. Bennett: That's right, I did say that and here is something else I want you to remember - "Writers need to be good readers - and some experts go as far to say that you must be a good reader to be a good writer!"

In this chapter you will read about:

The Characteristics of Excellent Readers

The Characteristics of Excellent Writers

Interesting Information about Reading and Writing

Ways to improve Reading and Writing with Content Area Exercises

The Important Basic Reading and Writing Terms and Concepts

The topic, main idea, topic sentence

The thesis statement

The Strategy: The 6 W Strategy

CHALLENGE 1

Becoming familiar with reading and writing concepts

Writing Connection

Before we continue, try writing a response to this statement:

"To be a good writer, you must be a good reader."

In at least two paragraphs, write some reasons why you believe or don't believe this to be true.

CHALLENGE 1

It's important to know some basic information about readers and writers

The characteristics of excellent readers:

- 👉 Read with a purpose
- 👉 Use prior knowledge to increase comprehension
- 👉 Are active—their minds are involved with the text
- 👉 Try to think in the same way the author wrote
- 👉 Keep expanding their vocabulary
- 👉 Know that not everything they read will be interesting
- 👉 Incorporate the 3 stages of reading: before, during, and after
- 👉 Read with a pencil
- 👉 Are willing to reread some sections several times
- 👉 Read with their eyes but interpret with their minds

The characteristics of excellent writers:

- 👍 Think about the audience and their reason or purpose for writing
- 👍 Have extended vocabularies and have acquired a lot of background information
- 👉 Take time to think before writing
- 👉 Are willing to revise and expect to make changes
- 👉 Know that becoming a good writer requires practice and discipline
- 👉 Are good listeners and observers
- 👉 Have lively imaginations
- 👉 Read a lot, especially the works of great writers

Does this describe you? Are you a good reader? Which one of these characteristics do you need to adopt? Highlight them

Does this describe you? Are you a good writer? Which one of these characteristics do you need to adopt? Highlight them

Interesting Information about Readers and Writers

- Readers and writers spend a lot of time reading and writing, they don't limit reading and writing activities only school assignments.

- Good Readers keep building vocabulary.

- Good readers think like good writers and good writers think like good readers.

- People are not born with reading and writing skills-they know they have to be developed.

- When people read, their knowledge base is expanded and when they write they use that base to express thoughts and ideas.

- A good way to improve one's writing is to study what other people have written.

- Understanding an author's message becomes more meaningful when you can write about it.

Important Basic Terms about Reading and Writing

Body paragraph:	All the paragraphs in an essay except for the introduction and conclusion are the "body paragraph." Each of those paragraphs supports the thesis.
Brainstorming:	Brainstorming is a prewriting activity. The writer makes a list of all the things that might relate to the topic within a five to ten minute time limit.
Conclusion:	The conclusion paragraph is the last or ending paragraph which restates the thesis.

Critical Thinking: Critical Thinking is a higher, more advanced level of thinking which goes beyond the basic, literal skills.

Drafting: Drafting is the "first draft" or first version of a paragraph or essay.

Freewriting: Freewriting is a prewriting activity in which the writer writes as much on a topic within a predetermined time limit.

Hook: A hook is the opening statement that grabs the reader's attention so the person will continue reading.

Introduction: The introduction is the first or beginning paragraph of an essay. The topic and usually the thesis statement appears in the introduction.

Journal: Journals are notebooks or computer files that writers use to jot down ideas, thoughts, and feelings about anything they are experiencing. Many times this information is used in their writings.

Main Idea: The main idea of a paragraph is the important point the author is making about the topic.

Mapping: Mapping, also known as clustering, is a prewriting activity which visually illustrates how a topic and details are connected to each other.

Paragraph: A paragraph is comprised of several sentences which support an idea or main idea. A paragraph can include a topic, main idea, topic sentence, supporting details, and transitions.

Pattern of Organization: Writers usually develop their ideas by using a pattern of organization. Commonly used patterns are narration, description, illustration, process, compare/contrast, classification, definition, cause-effect, and argument.

Plagarism: Using another writer's ideas or language without consent is plagiarism. It is cheating and a serious offense.

Prewriting: Prewriting is the beginning stage of writing. The author chooses a topic and then refines the topic with a strategy such as brainstorming, freewriting, questioning, mapping, or visualizing.

How many of these terms do you already know? Make sure you understand all the terms after you read these sections.

Purpose: The purpose of writing usually determines the words, style, and details. Common purposes are to entertain, to inform, and to persuade.

Supporting Details: Supporting details are the facts, examples, and details that explain and develop the main idea or thesis.

Thesis statement: An essay has a thesis statement which is the main idea or central thought.

Transitions: Transitions are the words or phrases that link ideas or concepts; they signal new, forthcoming information.

Visualizing: Visualizing is a prewriting activity in which the writer "pictures" the development of the essay. Often the reader "sketches" what has been visualized.

Writing Process: The Writing Process involves steps that writers use to assure completion of the writing project. The steps are: Previewing, Drafting, Revision, Editing, and Publishing.

Writing Connection

Before you begin Chapter Two, respond in writing to this prompt: "What makes me such a unique person?" Give yourself between 5 and 10 minutes to write the answer. After you have written the answer to the question, read your answer. Then write an answer to this question, "What can I do during the next few years to make myself a better person?"

The Reading and Writing Connection | 8

Chapter Summary

"If you want to learn something very well, read about it and then write about it." This method is a certain way to increase comprehension and retention because it requires that the reader must understand the intended message before writing about it - this gives assurance that the message was comprehended.

The 6 W Strategy: Who, What, Where, When, Why, and Who

"I keep six honest serving men (they taught me all I knew); their name are Who and What and Where and When and Why and Who."

Rudyard Kipling

Course: All courses

Goal: To learn basic information by asking the 6 W's

Material Needed: Textbook, class notes, handouts, notebook, pen or pencil

Individual or group: Individual

Lesson Duration: Varies

Finished Product to be graded: The 6 W Strategy can be applied to each concept in a chapter. Students can record answers to the 6 questions in a separate notebook that can be graded and also used for studying.

Why do I need to learn this?

Getting answers to the 6 W's is a dependable way to get the basic information about a topic you are studying. Notice that none of the interrogation words can be answered with one word. When learning something new, use these questions words as a guide.

Procedure

1. On a card or piece of paper, write the 6 question words so you can refer to them as you begin the strategy.

2. Identify the important concepts in each chapter. The concepts may be in the chapter overview, in the headings, in margins, in the syllabus or from your instructor.

3. In a notebook write a list of concepts. After reading about each concept write 6 questions for each concept. Ask Who, What, When, Where, Why, and Who. Write the answers next to the concept list. Some of the questions, such as "Who" and "When" may not apply to every concept.

4. Read your concept list and accompanying answers several times before your exam.

Final Thoughts

Newspaper journalists use the "6W" Strategy to guide them as they gather accurate facts for their news articles. After they have written the basic information, they can add details and additional information to expand the article.

2

Vocabulary

"Meaning is not in the words alone,
but is largely in the reader"

Edmund B. Huey, Psychologist
1817 -1913

Becoming A Great Reader and Writer In College

Read the introduction - Who will get the trip to Italy - Luis or John?

The PTA at the local high school has provided funds for a deserving high school senior to spend eight weeks in Italy during the summer. This fortunate person will study the Italian language and culture before beginning college in the fall. After reviewing the possible candidates, the PTA selected two students and now must make the final decision.

The candidates, Luis and John, are invited to meet with the PTA president. The president said the deciding factor would be based on an essay which is to be written in the next 45 minutes. Directions for the essay are: "Why do you think you should be awarded the summer trip to Italy? You have 45 minutes to complete this answer. The essay will be evaluated based on word usage (vocabulary) rather than content. Limit your essay to approximately 150 – 200 words."

Luis's Essay

I'm excited to have a chance to visit Italy and spend the summer learning the language and all about the culture. I have always loved to travel and I think I would be a very good candidate for many reasons.

First of all, I love everything about Italy, especially the paintings, sculptures, architecture, people, music, scenery, and all the ancient sites. Secondly, I would be able to experience Italy, not like a tourist, but as a student because I would be living like an Italian citizen for at least eight weeks.

The most important reason is that I would be able to learn about a culture that has contributed so much to the world. This knowledge would help me reach my long-term college goal which is to major in European history.

I appreciate that you are considering me for this opportunity. If I am selected, you will not be disappointed because I will be a good representative from our school and country. Thank you and thank all the PTA members.

John's Essay

I sincerely thank you for considering me to spend the summer in Italy. This will be an extraordinary opportunity to enrich my education. Being able to study in a historical, magnificent country will be a dream come true especially considering visiting Italy has always been a passion of mine.

In future years I will treasure the memories as I stroll along the Appian Way, ride in a gondola as the gondolier weaves his way through the maze of the Venetian waterways, meander through the charming villages, and gaze in awe at the art created by the Italian masters centuries ago.

Years from now I will cherish the unforgettable moments at the opera, the ambiance of local trattorias, the vineyards in the Tuscan countryside, and the lively conversations with the friendly shopkeepers. Yes, all these memories and unforgettable moments will be a lasting reminder of an exceptional summer.

The two months I spend in Italy will also provide a solid foundation for my intended college major, international business. Again, thank you for helping me pursue my studies. I promise to be the kind of representative for which our school and country can be proud of.

Which essay did you like the most? Most students say they like John's essay because he used a lot of descriptive words and phrases.

Underline "stroll along the Appian Way," "weaves his way through the maze of the Venetian waterways," "meander through the charming villages" and "gaze in amazement at the art." John's intention was to create vivid, visual images and to do that he wrote meander instead of "walk" weaves instead of "steers," or gaze instead of "look." By choosing the precise words, John's essay was an easy winner!"

What suggestions would you give Luis?

In this chapter you will read about:

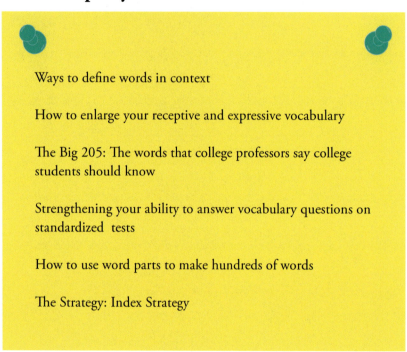

Ways to define words in context

How to enlarge your receptive and expressive vocabulary

The Big 205: The words that college professors say college students should know

Strengthening your ability to answer vocabulary questions on standardized tests

How to use word parts to make hundreds of words

The Strategy: Index Strategy

Quotes

"Don't tell me words don't matter. 'I have a dream.' Just Words? 'We hold these truths to be self-evident, that all men are created equal.' Just Words? ' We have nothing to fear but fear itself.' Just Words?"

Barack Obama, Milwaukee Wisconsin campaign speech
February 16, 2008

"Colors fade, temples crumble, empires fall but wise words endure."
Edward Thorndike, Psychologist
1874 - 1949

"How often misused words generate misleading thoughts."
Herbert Spencer, Philosopher
1820 -1903

"Words are, of course, the most powerful drug of mankind."
Rudyard Kipling, author and poet
1865-1936

Writing Connection

Respond: How does a college-level vocabulary contribute to comprehension for understanding reading, listening, spoken, and written expression? Use the quotes above to guide your response.

_____

_____

_____

Your vocabulary started with one word. It grew rapidly during the first six or seven years of your life. Some people continued to expand their vocabulary over the years while others moved more slowly in learning new words. Results of research and experience tell us that an extensive vocabulary is a characteristic of educated people.

The words you use create a self-portrait and a greater insight as to who you are. It's true that people will judge you by the words you use. A large vocabulary allows you to understand the thoughts of others through listening and reading. It's up to you to make sure you include vocabulary building during your college years.

Did you know that the English language has over one million words, yet average high school graduates only recognize about 50,000 words and use only 10,000 words when they speak and write? On the other hand, the average college graduates recognize about 70,000 words and use 20,000 words. Each day you will be exposed to new words in your classes and reading material. We present three challenges in this chapter to help you take advantage of this opportunity to learn new words.

CHALLENGE 1

Increasing expressive and receptive vocabularies: Focusing on the Big 205

The Expressive Vocabulary are all the words we use to "express" ourselves. They are the words we use when we speak, give oral presentations, or write an essay or report. We have an in-depth understanding of these words and have confidence in our ability to use them. The Expressive Vocabulary is smaller than the Receptive Vocabulary.

The Receptive Vocabulary are all the words we "receive" or take in when we read or listen. They're the words we read in textbooks, handouts, journals, novels, newspapers, or words we listen to in lectures and class discussions. The receptive vocabulary is quite large because we can take in or receive infinite numbers of words. Every day we hear or take in words from TV, the internet, text messages, music, conversations, lectures, books, newspapers, and other forms of written material.

When your parents talk to you, do you use your expressive or receptive vocabularies? Explain.

For example, the other day I read an article which used the word **disingenuous** *to describe a politician. I only had a superficial understanding of the word so it became a part of my Receptive Vocabulary. It's a word I "received" and until I feel confident using it when I speak or write, it will not become part of my expressive vocabulary.* **(disingenuous means dishonest)**

The three most widely used methods in college to learn receptive words are:

1) The Dictionary Method, 2) Using Context Clues and 3) Learning Word Parts

1. Dictionary Method
Looking up an unknown word in a dictionary has value, but also has a few drawbacks. Often an unknown word has many meanings and if the wrong meaning is selected, comprehension will be impaired. Furthermore, stopping to look up a word will disrupt reading.

2. Context Clues
This textbook favors learning vocabulary through context clues. Context clues are the other words in a sentence that help you to understand the meaning of a new word. The surrounding words in the sentence or in the paragraph give clues how to "figure out" an unfamiliar word's meaning.

How do you define words?

3. Learning Word Parts
Learning word parts means learning hundreds of prefixes, roots, and suffixes for the longer, multisyllabic words commonly found in college courses and textbooks.

👉 This chapter will increase your expressive and receptive vocabulary so you will have a large selection of college level words to use for oral presentations, writing assignments, listening, and reading.

👉 The Big 205 are words from college courses that professors said students should know. They are words you will want to learn in addition to the vocabulary from your classes, textbooks, and other resources.

👉 As a high school student your expressive vocabulary was probably on a high school level. You cannot assume that as you move through college your vocabulary will consistently increase and that at the end of four years, you will speak and write like a college graduate. Acquiring a college level vocabulary does not happen automatically or by chance. Most of the time it requires a systematic plan. So now here's the plan.

The Plan

👉 Learn the new academic words that you will encounter in your classes.

👉 Use these words in speaking and in writing.

👉 Know these words so well that they become second nature to you.

👉 Start to use these words beginning today and provide practice opportunities.

👉 Learn the Big 205 (pg 21). They are the college words you will encounter in your classes. Your professors will expect you to learn them - so, begin using them.

👉 Instead of looking up every word to fill out the Vocabulary Graph (page 21), "buddy up" by dividing the list among your classmates. Make a copy of the graph for everyone in your class. Then distribute and exchange copies with your classmates.

Making your own personal academic college dictionary

Assignment - Make a personal college vocabulary dictionary

Page 21 has the Big 205 academic vocabulary words that all students should acquire for their Expressive Vocabulary. These words are from lectures, class discussions and readings. Start using them when speaking and writing. You may recognize some of them but not know them well enough to use in conversation and/or writing. An efficient way to learn the words is to make a personal dictionary.

Tangible Dictionary

1. Divide the word list, Big 205, by the number of students in the class so each person is responsible for filling out the vocabulary graphs of 15-25 words or the number of words that can be evenly split between class members.

2. Use the Vocabulary Graph on page 21 and fill out the graph information for each word.

3. After the graphs are filled, make copies of your completed graphs for each student in the class.

4. Pass out your copies. Each student should assemble all vocabulary graphs in alphabetical order in a 3-ring binder.

5. Study these words and try to use as many as you can in conversations and in your writing.

6. Your professor will give a quiz on these words.

Electronic Dictionary

1. Divide the word list, Big 205, by the number of students in the class so each person is responsible for filling out the vocabulary graphs of 15 – 25 words or the number of words that can be split between class members.

2. Make an electronic copy of the vocabulary graph on page 21 and fill out the graph for each word assigned.

3. After the words are filled out electronically, send each member of the class a copy.

Remember, these words will help you throughout your college career and beyond. Try to use them when you speak and write.

4. Make a creative cover for your vocabulary book and place your word graphs and your classmates' word graphs in this file. Arrange the words in alphabetical order. Save it as a separate folder on your lap top and USB.

5. Study these words and use as many as you can in conversations and your writings.

6. Make sure you are very familiar with these words because your professor will give you a quiz on them.

Academic Vocabulary Words
The BIG 205

abridge	decimate	genteel	meander	recalcitrant
abyss	deductive	gratuitous	memoirs	redundancy
acrid	definitive	gregarious	mercurial	remorseful
advocate	delude	grievous	metropolis	reproach
aesthetic	denotation	gullible	mimicry	resilient
aghast	deprecate	gutteral	minutiae	revenge
agnostic	description	haphazard	mitigate	revoke
allusion	diaphonous	herculean	narcissism	rhetoric
ambiguity	dichotomy	hieroglyphics	neophyte	sarcasm
ambivalence	discord	homage	nonchalant	sardonic
amenable	disinclined	horde	noxious	scapegoat
analogy	divulge	hover	objective	secular
apathy	dour	idiom	omnipotent	segregate
assumption	duplicity	illicit	omniscient	somatic
astute	duress	imperil	ostracism	sporadic
autonomy	elucidate	implore	panacea	stereotype
bandanna	empathy	imply	paradox	subjective
benevolence	eminent	inane	paragon	subjugate
bequeath	emporium	incorrigible	pathos	succinct
biofeedback	enervate	inculcate	pejorative	suppression
boon	entree	inductive	penury	sycophant
bucolic	epicure	infer	perennial	taboos
candor	epitaph	inhibition	perfunctory	taciturn
cantankerous	epitome	innuendo	peripatetic	theory
capricious	erudite	insidious	perseverance	tirade
charlatan	ethics	intrepid	peruse	topography
chastise	etymology	introvert	placebos	tortuous
clandestine	euphemism	irony	plagiarism	transient
cliche'	exposition	jargon	posthumous	tryst
cognition	fallacy	jocularity	potpourri	validity
colloquial	fastidious	judicious	preposterous	vicarious
concur	feasible	juxtaposition	presumptuous	visage
condone	flaccid	latent	proclivity	wit
connive	flaunt	longevity	prodigious	
connotation	flout	maladaptive	profligate	
consensus	fortuitous	malefactor	prognosis	
contempt	frivolous	masochism	prudent	
convene	gargantuan	maudlin	quintessence	
culpable	generation	maxim	quixotic	

Print vocabulary word

Name: _____   Date: _____

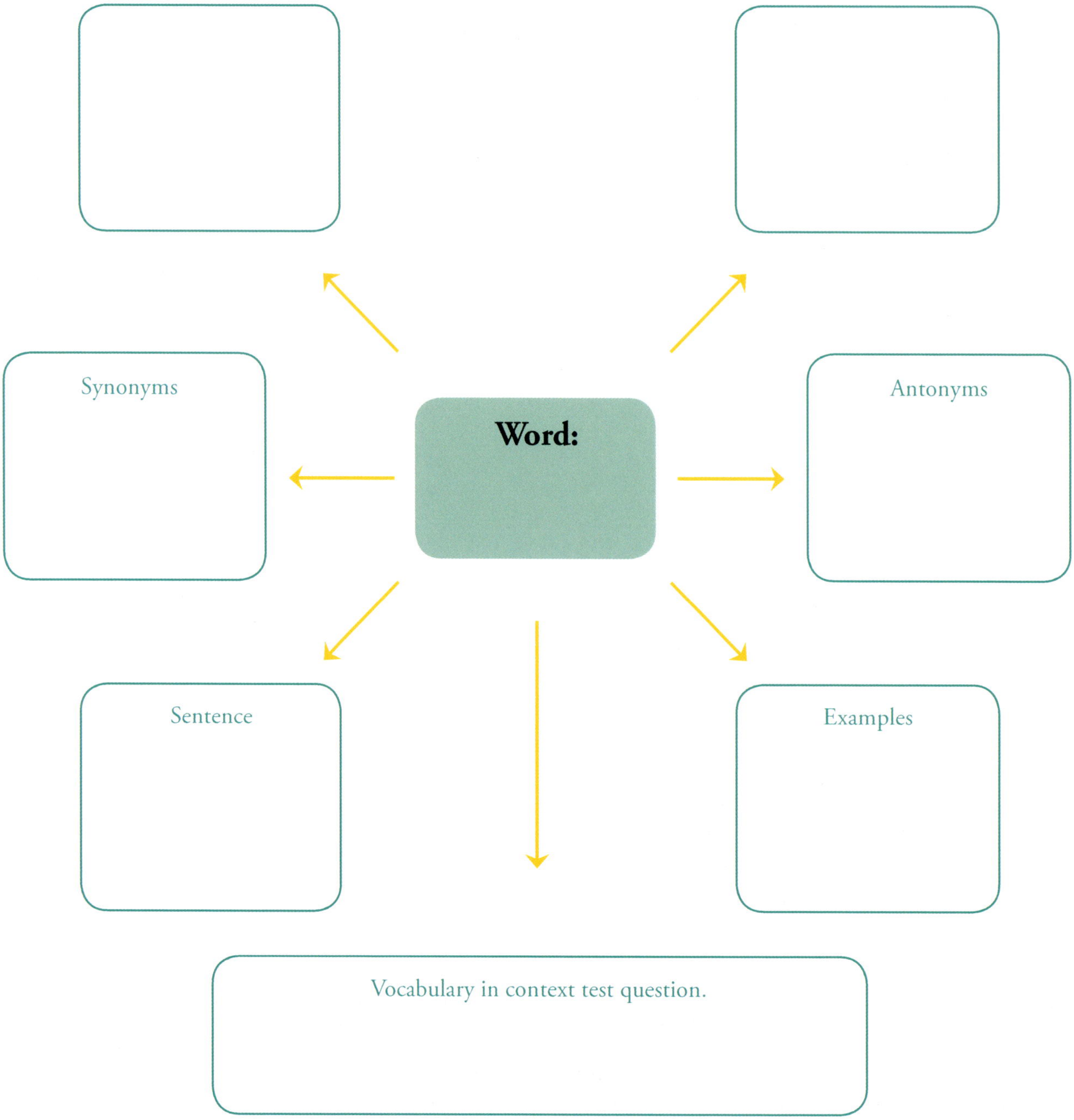

Synonyms

Antonyms

Word:

Sentence

Examples

Vocabulary in context test question.

CHALLENGE 2
Focusing on Context Clues
Defining context clues

Context clues are the "other" words in a sentence that help you understand the meaning of a new word. The surrounding words in the sentence or paragraph give cues how to "figure out" an unfamiliar word's meaning. For example, *"Many teachers leave their teaching career because they believe the **paltry** pay doesn't give them a middle-class lifestyle."*

The meaning of paltry becomes clear because the other words in the sentence suggest that the pay is low or insufficient.

"Context Clue Tips"

The next time you encounter a new word while reading... before opening a dictionary or glossary, continue reading to the end of the sentence or paragraph.

Stop for a moment and think about the meaning of the word.

With practice you will improve at predicting the meaning of new words. Overall, you will increase your vocabulary in an efficient and time saving way.

Five types of context clues: synonyms, antonyms, examples, general sense, and punctuation. Which type do you like best?

Examining the different types of context clues

1. Synonym Context Clues

One way authors define words in context is to use synonyms. The author uses a more familiar word with the same meaning to define or explain the word. This word may be in the same sentence as the unknown word or it may appear further along in the paragraph. **To define words in context, use synonyms as clues, and simply look for a word that has the same or similar meaning.**

Example: Gail's <u>fortuitous</u> lottery win allowed her to have a comfortable life. Most people do not get a chance to improve their financial status.

Explanation: In these sentences it is obvious *fortuitous* means chance or happening by chance. The synonym used is *chance* in the second sentence. It makes sense because lottery wins are by chance.

2. Antonym Context Clues

Antonyms are used in the same way as synonyms, but unlike synonyms, the author uses a word that is the opposite meaning in order to define or explain. A writer indicates a contrasting definition by using conjunctions which show differences between the term and the example or definition offered. **Clue words for antonyms are: but, yet, however, although, on the other hand, however, instead of, while, rather than, and on the contrary.** These words indicate that the author is continuing the discussion, but offering a contrasting term.

Example: We were all surprised that Gail married an <u>introvert</u> rather than someone who is very sociable, self-confident, and gregarious.

Explanation: We can see that the author continued his thought by contrasting the word <u>introvert</u> with the opposite meaning. The author used the clue "rather than" to indicate contrast. The meaning of <u>introvert</u> is the opposite of very sociable, self-confident, and having many outside interests.

3. Example Context Clues

Sometime the author has examples that give a full description of the term or point to be made. **In order to indicate that the author is giving an example that will help in defining the word or concept, the author might use terms such as: such as, for example, they are, for instance, including, pointing out, and involves.**

Example: During the early part of American history, drugstores sold tonics. These tonics were a <u>panacea</u> because they claimed to cure everything such as rheumatism, cancer, common cold, arthritis, heart disease, headaches, indigestion, and many other illnesses.

Explanation: It's clear that a <u>panacea </u>is a cure-all for everything because there are many examples to show the many illnesses that tonics can cure. The clue words, "such as", signal the list of illnesses.

4. General Sense Context Clues

Sometimes there are no synonyms, antonyms, or examples to provide clues to the word's meaning. In this case, you will have to understand the general sense of the passage in order to understand the meaning of the word. When the meaning is not stated in context, it is implied. **This means while you read you must use reasoning and common sense to define the word.** In order to develop the necessary background for a general sense type vocabulary in context, the writer may use the entire passage, or most of it.

Example: The school looked awful yesterday. By noon the hall was full of trash. Students who brought their fast food breakfast to school threw the paper wrappers and uneaten food into the garbage cans. But the cans could not hold all the trash, and paper and uneaten food littered the hallways. It had rained during the morning and students didn't bother to wipe their feet before entering the halls. When the principal arrived after his school board meeting, he looked at the mess and went into a <u>tirade</u> which could be heard throughout the school.

Explanation: In order to define <u>tirade</u>, use your general sense and common sense. The definition is in the paragraph, but it is implied. You can tell by the description of the hallway that the principal gave a long, angry speech criticizing the mess in the hall.

5. Punctuation Context Clues

Sometimes the meanings of words are set off by punctuation. **Meanings of words can be explicitly stated in context surrounded by parentheses, commas, or dashes within one sentence.**

Example: Henri's <u>gregarious</u> nature, noticeable friendliness, helps make him the type of candidate we want for mayor.

Explanation: You will notice that the definition of gregarious is set off with commas. <u>Gregarious</u> means noticeable friendliness.

Of the five major types of context clues, which one do you use?

Below are different context clues using the same word: gregarious

<u>Synonym Context Clues</u>
Henri's **gregarious** personality or noticeable **friendliness** should help him get elected.

<u>Antonym Context Clues</u>
Henri's **gregarious** personality will surely help him get elected because his opponent tends to be **withdrawn**.

<u>Example Context Clues</u>
Henri's **gregarious** nature should help win votes because his **good-natured, outgoing, friendly** personality will affect voters positively.

<u>General Sense Context Clues</u>
Henri's activities of **attending civic functions, shaking voter's hands, smiling, and displaying warmth,** shows his **gregarious** personality which should help get him elected.

<u>Punctuation Context Clues</u>
Henri's **gregarious** nature, **noticeable friendliness,** helps make him the candidate of choice.

Notice how punctuation helps in defining the word in context.

Bridging context clues and textbooks

<u>Assignment:</u> Look at the sentences below. They are examples of vocabulary in context using punctuation as clues. Read each example and find one like it in your content textbook. On the line beneath the example write the sentence from your content textbook and circle the definition. Be prepared to read your sentence to the class.

<u>Parentheses</u>
The <u>visage</u> (face or facial expression) on Carol's face indicated that she was surprised by the balloons and cake.

_____

_____

_____

Comma

The Duchess walked into the room, greeted everyone and nodded for dinner to be served in such a <u>genteel</u>, display of refinement and good manners, fashion.

_____

_____

Dash

Jeremy Schockey, tight end for the New Orleans Saints, planned to play in the 2010 Superbowl in spite of his knee injury sighting that he is <u>resilient</u> –able to recover quickly from setbacks.

_____

_____

Recognizing the limitations of context clues

Whenever possible, always try to use context clues for words you don't know. Using context clues is a recommended strategy because you won't have to interrupt your reading by looking up the word in a dictionary or thesaurus. Sometimes the exact meaning is not always in the context of the sentence or passage, but enough of the meaning should be there for you to understand without consulting a dictionary or thesaurus.

Keep in mind:

👉 *Writing is easy. All you have to do is cross out the wrong words.*

Mark Twain

👉 *Context clues rarely reveal the complete meaning.*

👉 *Context clues usually reveal only one meaning of ambiguous words.*

"When you're reading and come across a word you don't know it makes the reading very slow. So when you're assigned a difficult book make sure you don't overlook the long, unrecognizable, impossible words, the ones you have never seen or heard. It's going to be a really big problem if you are not able to pronounce them. So, before opening a dictionary, use the context clues. By doing this you will no longer be confused because the meaning will be clear to you. If you use the context, you will start to like reading-- and best of all, you'll understand the meaning."

Analyzing how correct and incorrect vocabulary questions are worded on standardized tests

On most tests, word meaning in context questions will come from passages in textbooks, independent writers, lectures, essays, newspapers, magazines, or made up by the text makers. The context clues can be located in the sentence of the word you want to define. The clues can also be found in the sentences before or after the sentence or somewhere else in the passage. The question may ask you to reread a particular sentence in the paragraph and define the underlined word. In other situations the student is instructed to define the underlined word.

Correct options:
A restatement or paraphrase of the definition of the word if the definition appears in the paragraph or sentence.
The definition of the word as it is used in a specific context.

Incorrect Options:

👉 A definition of the word that would be correct if the word were being used in another context;
Example: After surgery, most people shift into a **state** of consciousness.
Explanation: The most used definition of this word is the divided sections of our country, the United States, such as Florida. However, here it means a particular condition or status.

👉 A definition of the word that is sometimes confused with the word;
Example: I need one more principle.
Explanation: **Principle,** meaning standard, is often confused for "principal" such as a principal of a school.

👉 Words or phrases appearing in the passage that may be mistaken for the definition;
Example: Gail has been **persecuted** and found guilty by her classmates.
Explanation: Some students would choose guilty for the definition, however, persecuted means wronged or mistreated.

👉 Incorrect definition
Explanation: It is simply the wrong answer.

Ways context clues questions can be asked

1. The word_____in line_____in the passage means.
2. As used in line_____, the word_____means.
3. What is the meaning of_____as used in line_____.
4. Define the underlined words in the sentences below.

Reinforcing vocabulary in context through assignments

Writing Connection

Write a mini essay, 3 – 5 paragraphs, using ten of the Big 205 words. Use your personal dictionary to help. Choose a topic to write about:

☐ My summer vacation

☐ My favorite place to visit

☐ What makes a good professor

☐ A topic suggested by your professor.

Exercise 1: Vocabulary Multiple Choice

Choose a synonym for each word.

1. **potpourri**
a. arrangement   b. recipe   c. mixture   d. container

2. **candor**
a. embarrassment   b. frankness   c. flattery   d. dishonesty

3. **homage**
a. distinction   b. cheer   c. respect   d. reward

4. **mercurial**
a. element   b. changeable   c. festive   d. stable

5. **bucolic**
a. rural life   b. weathered   c. comfortable   d. restored

6. **euphemism**
a. more agreeable statement   b. synonym   c. expression   d. compliment

7. **cliché**
a. compliment   b. small hat   c. critical remark   d. trite phrase

8. **taciturn**
a. loafer   b. reserved   c. relaxed   d. talkative

9. **succinct**
a. replacement   b. to the point   c. long winded   d. alternate

10. **vicariously**
a. personally   b. indirectly   c. frequently   d. secretly

11. **epicure**
a. overachiever   b. gourmet   c. principal   d. entrepreneur

12. **sporadic**
a. irregular   b. frivolous   c. constant   d. fleeting

13. **gregarious**
a. generous   b. slovenly   c. sociable   d. logical

14. **maudlin**
a. unemotional   b. sentimental   c. immature   d. materialistic

15. **inhibition**
a. encouragement   b. injustice   c. considerate   d. self-consciousness

16. **latent**
a. obvious   b. concealed   c. long term   d. generous

17. **chastised**
a. disciplined   b. complimented   c. laughed at   d. glared

18. **ambivalent**
a. unwavering   b. contradictory   c. neighborly   d. immobile

19. **consensus**
a. opinion   b. fearlessness   c. difference of opinion   d. general agreement

20. **infer**
a. provoke   b. conclude   c. introduce   d. worry

Exercise 2: Vocabulary in Context

The same words in Exercise I are now used in a sentence. Select the correct meaning after reading the word in context. Compare answers with Exercise I.

1. I used all the spices in my cabinet to make the soup which gave it a wonderful *potpourri* of smells.
a. arrangement   b. recipe   c. mixture   d. receptacle

2. I know I asked for her opinion of my new swim suit but her *candor* made me wish I hadn't bought it.
a. embarrassment   b. frankness   c. flattery   d. dishonesty

3. The bronze medal was awarded to the wounded soldiers to pay *homage* for their heroism.
a. distinction   b. cheer   c. respect   d. reward

4. Her *mercurial* temperament ranges from sweetness to loud, vulgar language.
a. element   b. changeable   c. festive   d. stable

5. After a hectic, noisy week in the city, I anticipate a quiet weekend in my *bucolic* country cabin.
a. rural life   b. weathered   c. comfortable   d. restored

6. Please don't use the term, constant complainer. Can't you think of an *euphemism*?
 a. more agreeable term b. synonym   c. expression   d. compliment

7. I wish my teacher would choose another expression than to use the same *cliché*, "you can do better."
a. compliment   b. small hat   c. critical remark   d. trite phrase

8. I am sure my *taciturn* child has something to say during class discussion, but she rarely contributes anything.
a. noisy   b. reserved   c. relaxed   d. talkative

9. He is a man of few words because his *succinct* answers are correct but I wish he would say more.
a. replacement   b. to the point   c. long-winded   d. alternate

10. I was never able to afford the trip to see the pyramids in Egypt but *vicariously* I know all about them through my research.
a. personally   b. indirectly   c. frequently   d. secretly

11. She was a wonderful cook but after going to culinary school, she became an *epicure*.
a. overachiever   b. gourmet   c. principal   d. entrepreneur

12. The headaches were *sporadic* because she never knew when they would occur.
a. irregular   b. frivolous   c. constant   d. fleeting

13. Since he is *gregarious* by nature, he definitely should have a career in sales.
a. generous   b. slovenly   c. sociable   d. logical

14. I rarely ask my grandmother about the good old days because she becomes weepy and *maudlin*.
a. unemotional   b. sentimental   c. immature   d. materialistic

15. I always thought May was shy and reserved until I saw that she lost all *inhibition* in her first stage appearance.
a. encouragement   b. injustice   c. consideration   d. self-consciousness

16. Although I wish I could be completely honest, my true feelings are *latent* or hidden from everyone.
a. obvious   b. concealed   c. long-term   d. generous

17. My grandmother *chastised* me for wearing jeans, a tank top, and flip-flops to her birthday party.
a. disciplined   b. complimented   c. laughed at   d. glared

18. I wish my parents would stop being so *ambivalent* and decide if I can go to the expensive college.
 a. unwavering   b. contradictory   c. neighborly   d. immobile

19. It's fun to do homework with my group of friends because we choose answers based on *consensus*.
 a. opinion   b. fearlessness   c. difference of opinion   d. general agreement

20. Just because I'm six foot ten inches, don't *infer* that I will be a basketball player.
 a. provoke   b. conclude   c. introduce   d. worry

Exercise 3: Context Clues: Synonyms

Choose the word or term that means the same as the italicized word.

1. The class clown who went to great lengths to gain attention, made some inane or foolish remarks about our principal.
Inane means: _____

2. Mom is so agreeable, because she concurs with my decision to live in the dorms.
Concurs means: _____

3. The helicopter looked as though it was suspended in air as it hovered over the crime scene.
Hovered means: _____

4. His sensible judgment convinced me he would be a very judicious member.
Judicious means: _____

5. The special language used by the carnival workers sounded like jargon.
Jargon means: _____

6. She can be such a bore because she mainly talks about minutiae such as insignificant details, and unimportant topics.
Minutiae means: _____

7. We warned her that when she wore the sheer dress she had better wear a slip because the fabric of the dress was diaphanous.
Diaphanous means: _____

8. The car was filled with noxious fumes which we thought would be very harmful to one's health.
Noxious means: _____

Exercise 4: Context Clues: Antonyms

Find a word or term that means the opposite as the italicized word and then write the meaning of the italicized word.

1. She is an *introvert*, not like her outgoing, extroverted brother.
Introvert means: _____

2. Mary's *apathy* toward sky diving was in sharp contrast to my enthusiasm.
Apathy means: _____

3. It was a *blatant* lie, one that could not go unnoticed.
Blatant means: _____

4. The recruiter thought her appearance was too lax, he preferred a *fastidious* image.
Fastidious means: _____

5. Why did you *abridge* your original lengthy poem?
Abridge means:_____

6. Every summer *hordes* of mosquitoes invaded our yard, but in the winter only a few come.
Hordes means: _____

7. Your closet should be well-organized and not look like this *haphazard* mess.
Haphazard means: _____

8. I prefer to be somewhat *gullible*, rather than always being suspicious of everything.
Gullible means: _____

Exercise 5: Context Clues: Example

1. By showing the similarities between horseracing and dog racing, it was clear that everyone understood the basics of training. For example, she used an *analogy* approach to explain training for distance and for sprints.
Analogy means: _____

2. His subtle *innuendos* which included suggestions, smiles, and hints convinced the judge.
Innuendos means: _____

3. The comedian's wit was full of humorous *jocularity*.
Jocularity means: _____

4. I was offended by his *sarcasm*, especially his cutting, bitter remarks about my family.
Sarcasm means: _____

5. The child had a gloomy, *dour* appearance that included an unfriendly, frowning face.
Dour means: _____

6. Even though he has had so many disasters and catastrophes in his young life, he is *resilient* and usually bounces back.
Resilient means: _____

7. The principal recommended a strict boarding school for the *incorrigible* boy because the discipline would be severe and reinforcing.
Incorrigible means: _____

8. Each year the town is full of *transient* visitors who bring in a lot of money for the town's economy.
Transient means: _____

Exercise 6: Context Clues: General Sense

Write the meaning of the italicized word based on the context.

The *flaccid* branches on the orange trees worried the Florida fruit farmers. The frost that lasted three weeks was blamed for the trouble. Many orange trees died. But, at the first sign of warm weather, farmers looked for ways to *fortify* their orange groves with firm branches that hold plump round oranges.

1. The word *flaccid* in this paragraph means
      a. drooping and lifeless
      b. cup
      c. firm
      d. brownish green

2. To *fortify* is to
      a. begin a construction project
      b. strengthen
      c. body structure
      d. form or develop

He was the type of CEO that relished employees who acted like *sycophants*. He never wanted the intellectuals around him although he picked their brains for guidance and ideas. But, it was these intellectuals who represented the company abroad and at social functions quickly gained attention for their *wit*. But, everyone knew the *longevity* for a career with the company did not belong to the intellectual but to those who kept praising the boss.

3. The word *sycophant* means
    a. someone who is consistently sick
    b. an intellectual who gains power due to his strengths and knowledge of the job
    c. a servile or obsequious person who flatters somebody powerful for personal gain
    d. someone who is not smart

4. *Wit* can mean shrewdness. In this context it means
    a. agreeableness
    b. the ability to confuse people
    c. the ability to quickly close a business deal
    d. kindness

5. *Longevity* means
    a. long life
    b. elongated
    c. probability
    d. the length of somebody's employment or career.

The teacher watched the 11th graders' face as they viewed a video of the school's football players fighting the opposing team. The school's football team punched and kicked the players at moments when the referee was not watching. The teacher told the class that she does not *condone* such behavior. She continued by saying that the class had absolutely no *empathy* for the opposing team. The team was punched and kicked at unexpected moments.

6. *condone* means
    a. make allowances for or ignore
    b. punish
    c. an athletic procedure
    d. the act of being nice

7. *empathy* means
    a. sympathy
    b. fever due to a severe cold
    c. ability to understand and identify with someone else's feelings
    d. ability to take matters into our own hands and make a decision

Driving through the Appalachian Mountains turned out to be such a long *tortuous* drive. It was the beginning of the summer so the leaves and foliage began to look beautiful. It appeared that Mother Nature was *flaunting* the good she can do because of the damage she did during the winter.

8. *tortuous* means
    a. to torture
    b. twisting and twining
    c. complex
    d. straight

9. *flaunting* means
    a. playful actions
    b. To show something off
    c. a dessert made of cream
    d. failing

Exercise 7: Homework/Practice: Use the context and write the meaning of the italicized word

1. The homeless man owned nothing and lived in *penury* but had a dream that one day he would live in luxury.
Penury: _____

2. As a *neophyte* trying to learn jazz piano by myself, I finally had to hire an expert.
Neophyte: _____

3. Losing her parents was a *grievous* loss and certainly the saddest, most heartbreaking occurrence in her life.
Grievous: _____

4. I feel very *remorseful* after I said those unkind words to my sister.
Remorseful: _____

5. After the family lost their house, the father became *prudent* and insisted each person in the house contribute a few dollars a week into the family fund.
Prudent: _____

6. He would never embezzle the money, he has a *scrupulous* reputation.
Scrupulous: _____

7. Because the teacher was constantly late, she was severely *reproached* by the principal in a most critical way.
Reproached: _____

8. Unfortunately, she has a *proclivity* toward rich, fattening desserts.
Proclivity: _____

9. I never knew if my friend's remarks are sincere because she is known for her *irony.*
Irony: _____

10. He maybe *deluding* himself but he thinks he will be chosen in the first or second round.
Deluding: _____

11. Since the students disagree on everything, there is *discord* and no compatibility with anyone.
Discord: _____

12. It was an old fashioned *emporium*, a department store that carried most everything.
Emporium: _____

13. The grandfather could not help that his voice was husky and *guttural*; unfortunately, he scared his granddaughter.
Guttural: _____

14. The only way to *mitigate* the headache was three aspirins and a nap.
Mitigate: _____

15. We were completely *aghast* when seeing the city after the earthquake.
Aghast: _____

16. The jeweler *bequeathed* his most precious gems to his daughters and not his sons.
Bequeathed: _____

17. I *advocate* five hours a week of community service for all high school students and oppose anyone suggesting otherwise.
Advocate: _____

18. The *redundancy* of his speech made it boring and made me wonder why he couldn't deliver just the important information.
Redundancy: _____

19. In our search for the cast, we found Mrs. Brown who fit the *stereotype* of the perfect grandmother.
Stereotype: _____

20. The current ban on smoking should not be *revoked* even though smokers want it restored.
Revoked: _____

Exercise 8: Test I

Use the context and select the correct meaning for each word.

1. We received **sanction** to proceed with the building plans because everything was in order.
  a. advisement   b. recommendation   c. approval   d. encouragement

2. Jefferson was one of our founder's most **eminent** statesmen.
  a. undistinguished   b. high ranking   c. domineering   d. devoted

3. My friend is atypical of most young mothers because she shows only **spasmodic** bursts of affection toward her young children.
  a. small   b. abrupt   c. steady   d. occasional

4. The **transgressor** couldn't understand why he was given a forty year sentence and the innocent one couldn't understand why he didn't receive compensation.
  a. offender   b. innocent person   c. fugitive   d. complainer

5. The reason for her **colloquialism** was because she was homeschooled and never had the benefit of formal language instruction.
  a. exuberance   b. demeanor   c. slang   d. precision

6. Her beauty set the standard for the **epitome** that every casting director wanted for Beauty and the Beast.
  a. fairness   b. model   c. enjoyment   d. resplendence

7. Walking three miles in the strong sun **enervated** my strength and made me very weary.
  a. exhausted   b. vitalized   c. replenished   d. soothed

8. My aunts have always been an example or **paragon** of lovely, gracious women.
  a. fusion   b. contradiction   c. compromise   d. prototype

9. It's not **feasible** to travel to Alaska in January.
  a. practical   b. perceptive   c. spectacular   d. stimulating

10. Listening to the opera brought forth so much **pathos** that I couldn't help weeping all through it.
  a. irony   b. creativity   c. sentiment   d. distress

11. He became an **agnostic** after he saw years and years of suffering in the third world country.
  a. doubter   b. agitator   c. believer   d. troublemaker

12. The karate instructor *chastised* me for arriving late.
a. disciplined   b. complimented   c. warned   d. embarrassed

13. The summary notes at the end of the chapter *elucidated* the text's message so I finally understood.
a. confused   b. clarified   c. contradicted   d. dominated

14. It's a *fallacy* that everyone needs eight hours of sleep every night.
a. fact   b. obligation   c. belief   d. misconception

15. When I won a hundred dollars in the lottery, I decided to buy something *frivolous* for myself.
a. sensible   b. impractical   c. economical   d. overpriced

16. Her *narcissistic* behavior is obvious to everyone when they see her admiring herself in every mirror she passes.
a. self-centered   b. unselfish   c. sophisticated   d. natural

17. My sister is a *chronic* complainer when she sees people talking on the phone and driving at the same time.
a. temporary   b. persistent   c. lively   d. bad-tempered

18. My roommate and I had a *tacit* agreement that we would turn out the lights before midnight.
a. delightful   b. wordy   c. natural   d. understood

19. Her giggle was the last *vestige* of her childhood.
a. discovery   b. figure of speech   c. lingo   d. evidence

20. I needed to *peruse* the letter slowly and read between the lines to realize he wanted to end the relationship.
a. read carefully   b. read out loud   c. cling to   d. relinquish

21. You had better hire an *astute* tax lawyer for this complicated tax situation you have.
a. refined   b. unknowing   c. articulate   d. shrewd

22. It was a formal, black tie affair hosted by the most *genteel* couple I had ever known.
a. gentle   b. powerful   c. refined   d. boorish

23. The old town had windy streets so I enjoyed *meandering* through them all afternoon.
a. going directly   b. jogging   c. biking   d. wandering

24. Students who buy research papers online are *culpable* of cheating and may face expulsion.
a. guilty   b. insensitive   c. blameless   d. capable

25. My host gave me a *perfunctory* hello which did not make me feel welcome.
 a. phony   b. aggressive   c. indifferent   d. two-faced

26. It's a *paradox*—the more money he makes, the cheaper he becomes.
 a. rule   b. inconsistency   c. tribute   d. fact

27. Despite her injury she always had a *perennial* smile on her face.
 a. fascinating   b. occasional   c. permanent   d. thoughtful

28. He failed all his midterms; how can he be so *nonchalant?*
 a. smug   b. unconcerned   c.sorrowful   d. fascinating

29. After my parents explained the situation, I could see their *valid* argument.
 a. intense   b. oblivious   c. inaccurate   d. acceptable

30. My mother is *cantankerous* when she enters my very untidy bedroom.
 a. ill-tempered   b. fascinated   c. domineering   d. mellow

Exercise 9: Test II: Vocabulary in Context

Read selection and using context clues, circle the best meaning for italicized words.

An Incomparable Book Club

Prior to the 1990's many people's perceptions of Book Clubs were that they were primarily for members who were *erudite* intellectuals who *convened* and discussed books. These clubs typically depended on newspapers and magazines to review and recommend newly published books to see what would be on interest to their members.

All that changed on September 17, 1996 when Oprah Winfrey *divulged* that everyone would be invited to join Oprah's Book Club. Her *objective* was to create a Book Club for everyone so people's lives all over the world would be enriched by the written word. Oprah's words, "I love books! I think books open windows to the world for all of us." These *candid* remarks did more to advance literacy than all the *imploring* words promoted by reading teachers in the last fifty years. The members had confidence in Oprah's selections.

To put it mildly, Oprah's Book Club, like so many of her other endeavors has had *prodigious* success. Today there are approximately two million members. Not only do these members receive well-written, entertaining, "Oprah selected books" but they also have *entrée* to in-depth study guides and expert question and answer websites where they can connect with other online members.

The influence of Oprah's Book Club defied conventional wisdom. Many people predicted the demise of the book industry because of the pervasiveness of online resources. Former *disinclined* readers now spend time reading. Book sales have been a boon to publishers and people who otherwise might never have *perused* a book are now socially engaged in interpreting books. Oprah has also been responsible for the success of otherwise *obscure* writers. Like so many of Oprah's accomplishments, the Book Club has touched, and even changed many people's lives.

1. **Erudite**
a. well-educated   b. shallow   c. important   d. refined

2. **Convened**
a. performed   b. started   c. gathered together   d. understood

3. **Divulged**
a. concealed   b. made known   c. exclaimed   d. indicated

4. **Objective**
a. existence   b. exclamation   c. goal   d. choice

5. **Candid**
a. casual   b. amenable   c. tedious   d. honest

6. **Imploring**
a. connecting   b. urging   c. summarizing   d. asking

7. **Prodigious**
a. exceptional   b. versatile   c. exquisite   d. meager

8. **Entrée**
a. opportunity   b. attractiveness   c. admittance   d. authority

9. **Disinclined**
a. discriminating   b. reluctant   c. withdrawn   d. inferior

10. **Boon**
a. benefit   b. accomplishment   c. relief   d. responsibility

11. **Perused**
a. handled   b. purchased   c. enjoyed   d. read

12. **Obscure**
a. popular   b. unknown   c. published   d. dull

Challenge 3: Using word parts to build hundreds of words

Jeremy, a former student of mine, has always been a bibliophile and now wants to become a lexicographer! It's easy to see that Jeremy loves books (biblio means books) (phil means love) and wants to become an author or editor of a dictionary (lex means word) (cog means to know) and (graph means to write.)

He is always combining prefixes, roots, and suffixes to form long, interesting, and creative words. Jeremy just told me he received a perfect score on the verbal portions of the SAT. When I asked him if he would share his list of the most important word parts, he didn't hesitate at all. So, in this chapter, we will teach you the prefixes, suffixes, and roots that our friend, Jeremy, said should be learned.

Meeting Challenge 3: Using Word Parts to Build Hundreds of Words

👉 Learn the basics of word parts

👉 Take a pre-test of common word parts

👉 Learn about two powerful tools

👉 Practice what you learned by completing exercises 1-5

👉 Take the post-test of common word parts

We see word parts all the time; they can help in understanding the meaning of words

Introduction to Word Parts

Now that you are advancing in school, you have probably noticed that the new vocabulary words and terms are much longer. Many words have more than three syllables - they are often difficult to pronounce, and you may not know the meaning!

Most of the longer words are made of prefixes, roots, and suffixes. These words begin with a prefix or two you may already know. For example, the word philanthropy. You may remember from reading about Jeremy on the preceding page that **phile (from bibliophile)** means love. So, philanthropy has something to do with love. You will learn that the root **anthro** means **mankind** so if you put love and mankind together as in philanthropy, you will know that this word means the **love of mankind or goodwill.**

If you cannot determine the meaning of a word part, think of a word you understand that has that word part and use this known word as a hint to the meaning

Another example is the word pericardium. In math you know the word perimeter means the distance around so pericardium means the distance around something. You will learn that cardio or cardium means the heart (as in cardiologist) so if you put "around" and "heart" together as in pericardium, you will know that this word means something that surrounds or is around the heart. **Knowing about 50 word parts will yield thousands of words!**

Learn the common word parts
Exercise 1: Take the Pre-test of word parts

Circle the best meaning for the word part. Check your answers on page 226. Use an index card and write the word part that you got wrong on one side and the correct meaning on the other side and a few synonyms. Review the cards often because you will be taking a post test at the end of this chapter.

1. **Acro**
   a. strong   b. highest   c. athletic   d. gymnast

2. **Ante**
   a. relative   b. before   c. later   d. during

3. **Anti**
   a. for   b. hatred   c. against   d. other

4. **Audi**
   a. hear   b. car   c. pain   d. ache

5. **Auto**
   a. type of car   b. self   c. highway   d. transportation

6. **Bene**
   a. beginning   b. sincere   c. harmful   d. good

7. **Bi**
   a. two   b. division   c. against   d. many

8. **Bio**
   a. story   b. scene   c. life   d. book

9. **Cent**
   a. money   b. sensation   c. one hundred   d. contest

10. Chron
    a. time   b. color   c. watch   d. circle

11. Cogn
    a. live   b. know   c. read   d. memory

12. Cycl
    a. circle   b. machine   c. cyclone   d. series

13. Dec
    a. card game   b. platform   c. ten   d. series

14. Demos
    a. waste   b. clouds   c. curve   d.people

15. Dia
    a. through   b. next to   c. solid   d. on top of

16. Dis
    a. bad   b. not   c. argue   d. outside

17. Ex
    a. different   b. beyond   c. out   d. outside

18. Fin
    a. steady   b. end   c. free   d. fix

19. Graph
    a. comical   b. write   c. picture   d. photograph

20. Grat
    a. please/thank b. letter   c. note   d. grated

21. Greg
    a. heavy   b. different   c. herd   d. not know

22. Hyper
    a. sleep   b. know   c. cluster   d. over, above

23. Hypo
    a. young   b. under, below c. water   d. blood

24. Hydro
    a. health   b. harmony   c. sacred   d. water

25. **Lav**
   a. praise   b. extend   c. free   d. wash

26. **Mal**
   a. bad   b. content   c. place   d. light

27. **Micro**
   a. star   b. middle   c. small   d. huge

28. **Migr**
   a. break   b. move   c. spark   d. place

29. **Mis**
   a. wrong   b. first   c. beyond   d. into

30. **Neo**
   a. old   b. new   c. antique   d. below

31. **Omni**
   a. over   b. equal   c. forever   d. all

32. **Pac**
   a. please,peace   b. bread   c. equal   d. wealth

33. **Para**
   a. middle   b. beyond   c. alongside   d. parents

34. **Patri**
   a. father   b. warning   c. speech   d. speak

35. **Peri**
   a. to feel   b. around   c. swing   d. inside

36. **Phil**
   a. show   b. love   c. father   d. sight

37. **Phobia**
   a. light   b. fear   c. power   d. hateful

38. **Phon**
   a. near   b. city   c. sound   d. words

39. **Poly**
    a. many   b. few   c. oil   d. city

40. **Post**
    a. letter   b. office   c. after   d. mind

41. **Pre**
    a. after   b. before   c. next   d. school

42. **Pseudo**
    a. like   b. false   c. name   d. clothes

43. **Rupt**
    a. volcano   b. itch   c. break   d. fall

44. **Spec**
    a. family   b. mark   c. look   d. end

45. **Sub**
    a. under   b. above   c. large   d. water

46. **Terra**
    a. patio   b. earth   c. animal   d. paper

47. **Thermos**
    a. winter   b. cold   c. heat   d. giant

48. **Trans**
    a. wind   b. across   c. train   d. turn

49. **Uni**
    a. one   b. country   c. twist   d. college

50. **Vert**
    a. carry   b. line   c. turn   d. color

What are the three kinds of word parts?

Prefix

A prefix comes before the root and it tells more about the root and causes a change in meaning.

Root

A root is the basic part or core of the word. It hold the basic meaning of the word.

Suffix

A suffix comes at the end of the word. It alters the meaning and the way the word is used in the sentence.

What are word families?

Word families have the same root or the same prefix.
Antifreeze, antisocial, and **antiseptic** have the same prefix (**anti**) which means against.

Migratory, migrant, and **immigrate** have the same root (**migr**) which means to move.

What are the two most powerful tools to increase your vocabulary?

Dictionaries

A dictionary is one of the most powerful learning tools you'll ever use in school. It is always in style and you can keep it for a lifetime. (Put this on your Christmas list.)

<u>Learn the different types of dictionaries</u>
A **pocket dictionary** is a small, lightweight book with about 15,000 words and short definitions. You can mark the words you look up and carry it around with you so you can use it in class. Any time you have to wait, such as waiting for a bus, you can take it out and review the words you marked.

An **abridged dictionary** is shortened or condensed version of the large **unabridged dictionary**—the kind you find in the reference section of the library. The abridged dictionary has about 150,000 words. Three abridged dictionaries favored by experts are: Merriam-Webster Collegiate Dictionary, American Heritage College Dictionary, and Random House Webster's College Dictionary.

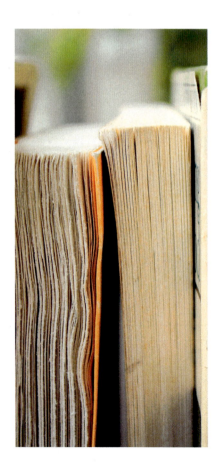

Each word in a dictionary
👉 Informs you how to pronounce the word

👉 Shows how the word is divided into syllables

👉 Gives the origin or etymology of the word

👉 Gives definition(s)

👉 Shows the related forms of the word

👉 Gives the parts of speech

👉 Shows the synonyms and antonyms and often has a sentence using the word

Thesaurus

The word thesaurus means treasure. It is a dictionary of synonyms and antonyms.

Since the English language has over a million words, there are many, many synonyms and antonyms for most words. For example, if you look up the word "bright" in a thesaurus, you will get at least 50 synonyms all having a different shade of meaning. A few of the synonyms are brilliant, radiant, shimmering, vivid, and glittering. You will also get a selection of antonyms.

A thesaurus is a valuable resource to use when writing. The most widely used is Roget's Thesaurus.

We recommend that during college you need to buy a pocket dictionary, an abridged dictionary (for your desk) and a thesaurus. Investing in these three extraordinary tools will help you become the student you want to become. With continued use as you use these tools to read, study, and write, you will begin to notice you are replacing the overused, worn out words with words having more expressive, precise meanings. As you become more word conscious, you will start feeling more confident as the words become part of your expressive vocabulary. You will also begin to notice the effect your expanding vocabulary has on others.

Online dictionaries and thesauruses and other reference material

An online dictionary and thesaurus are very convenient to use, however, it is advisable to also have a hard copy of the pocket dictionary, abridged dictionary, and thesaurus. The main reason is that you cannot write on an online dictionary. Writing in a book has a positive effect on learning and retaining information.

All the words I use in my stories can be found in the dictionary—it's just a matter of arranging them into the right sentences.
Somerset Maugham

Exercise 2: Self-Test Make sure you know the important information in this chapter.

1. What are the 3 word parts?

2. What does the word thesaurus mean?

3. Name 2 dictionaries. Which one is recommended to take to class?

4. Name 2 more words in the same family as produce.

5. What profession do lexicographers have?

Exercise #3: Find one or two words for each word part from Exercise 1. Feel free to consult a dictionary or thesaurus.

_____

_____

_____

_____

_____

_____

_____

Exercise #4: Match a word part from Column A with its meaning from Column B.

List 1

Col A	Col B
1. Peri ____	a. ten
2. Trans ____	b. under
3. Cent ____	c. one hundred
4. Fin ____	d. wheel, circle
5. Sub ____	e. sound
6. Uni ____	f. around
7. Cycl ____	g. one
8. Phon ____	h. across
9. Dec ____	i. end
10. Bi ____	j. two

List 2

Col A	Col B
1. Chron ____	a. after
2. Biblio ____	b. life
3. Bio ____	c. father
4. Pac ____	d. new
5. Rupt ____	e. time
6. Post ____	f. peace
7. Ante ____	g. please, thank
8. Neo ____	h. break
9. Grat ____	i. book
10. Patri ____	j. before

List 3

Col A	Col B
1. Pan ____	a. do, make
2. Proto ____	b. tooth
3. Retro ____	c. all
4. Phil ____	d. measure
5. Dent ____	e. different
6. Meter ____	f. same
7. Fac ____	g. first
8. Homo ____	h. backward
9. Ten ____	i. love
10. Hetro ____	j. hold, keep

List 4

Col A	Col B
1. Ex ____	a. under
2. Pre ____	b. small
3. Micro ____	c. forward
4. Mono ____	d. write
5. Pro ____	e. eight
6. Oct ____	f. before
7. Graph ____	g. over, beyond
8. Hypo ____	h. fear
9. Hyper ____	i. out of
10. Phobia ____	j. one

List 5

Col A	Col B
1. Ver, vert ____	a. hear
2. Mal ____	b. see, look
3. Bene ____	c. people
4. Audi ____	d. heat
5. Thermos ____	e. many
6. Spect ____	f. turn
7. Auto ____	g. good
8. Poly ____	h. easy
9. Demos ____	i. bad
10. Facil ____	j. self

List 6

Col A	Col B
1. Para ____	a. know
2. Cogn ____	b. wash
3. Pseudo ____	c. heard, sociable
4. Acro ____	d. through
5. Migr ____	e. false
6. Lav ____	f. all
7. Omni ____	g. along side
8. Greg ____	h. highest
9. Dia ____	i. move
10. Bio ____	j. life

Exercise #5: Make words combining prefixes, roots, and suffixes - "the building blocks" to make new words. In some cases, you may have to add or delete a letter.

Prefixes	Roots	Suffixes
1. Dia (through)	15. Phobia (fear)	33. Ic
2. Sub (under)	16. Cap (take, seize)	34. Arch
3. Hypo (under)	17. Ego (I, self)	35. Logy
4. Peri (around)	18. Auto (self)	36. Sion
5. Re (back)	19. Chrono, chron (time)	37. Tion
6. Tele (far)	20. Demo (people)	38. Ion
7. Bi (two, twice)	21. Hydro (water)	39. Ism
8. Anti (against)	22. Meter, metero (measure)	40. Y
9. Com (with, together)	23. Phon, phono (sound)	41. Ible
10. Con (with, together)	24. Cred (believe)	42. Able
11. Col (with, together)	25. Dic, dict (say, speak)	
12. Pre (before)	26. Spec, spect (see)	
13. Mono (one)	27. Ver, vers, vert (turn)	
14. Epi (over, above)	28. Voc (call)	
	29. Graph (write)	
	30. Poly (amy)	
	31. Derm, derma (skin)	
	32. Contra (against)	

The numbers below indicate the above listed prefix, suffix and root word part. Use the numbers below to identify which prefix, root and suffix to combine. Then combine the prefixes, roots, and suffixes to build new words. You may need to add or delete a letter for the new word. For example, in number one which is done for you, 21 on the list above is hydo and 35 on the list above is logy.

1. **21 + 35** = _hydrology_

2. **24 + 41** = _____

3. **5 + 26** = _____

4. **21 + 15** = _____

5. **16 + 37** = _____

6. **32 + 25** = _____

7. **4 + 22** = _____

8. **6 + 29** = _____

9. **3 + 31 + 33** = _____

10. **13 + 34** = _____

11. **27 + 36** = _____

12. **12 + 25+ 37** = _____

13. **6 + 23** = _____

14. **30 + 29** = _____

15. **13 + 29** = _____

16. **5 + 26 + 42** = _____

17. **23 + 29** = _____

18. **1 + 22** = _____

19. **19 + 35** = _____

20. **17 + 39** = _____

21. **10 + 27** = _____

22. **22 + 35** = _____

23. **20 + 29 + 33** = _____

24. **2 + 27 + 36** = _____

Exercise #6: Use the prefixes, roots, and suffixes from Exercise 5 to complete the words. Remember the numbers identify which word part to use.

1. **7 + ceps** _____

2. **3 + ten + 36** _____

3. **32 + st** _____

4. **5 + flec + 37** _____

5. **18 + mat + 33** _____

6. **9 + bus + 37** _____

7. **9 + fort + 42** _____

8. **26 + rum** _____

9. **11 + lec + 37** _____

10. **11 + on + 40** _____

11. **8 + bod + 40** _____

12. **8 + 7 + ot + 33** _____

13. **13 + tone** _____

14. **27 + atile** _____

15. **7 + lateral** _____

16. **20 + crat + 33** _____

17. **in + 24 + 41** _____

18. **bio + 29 + 40** _____

19. **21 + plane** _____

20. **12 + scrip + 37** _____

21. **geo + 35** _____

22. **photo + 29 + 33** _____

23. **geo + 29 + 40** _____

24. **extro + 27** _____

25. **10 + fu + 36** _____

Exercise 7: Post Test
Have you learned the word parts? Check answers on page 226

1. **post**

    a. letter   b. office   c. after   d. mind

2. **pre**

    a. after   b. before   c. next   d. school

3. **pseudo**

    a. like   b. false   c. name   d. clothes

4. **rupt**

    a. itch   b. volcano   c. break   d. fall

5. **spec**

    a. family   b. mark   c. look   d. end

6. **sub**

    a. under   b. above   c. large   d. water

7. **terra**

    a. patio   b. earth   c. animal   d. paper

8. **thermos**

    a. winter   b. cold   c. heat   d. giant

9. **trans**

    a. wind   b. across   c. train   d. turn

10. **uni**

    a. one   b. country   c. twist   d. cut

11. **vert**

    a. carry   b. line   c. entire   d. turn

12. **acro**

    a. strong   b. highest   c. athletic   d. gymnast

13. **ante**
    a. relative   b. before   c. later   d. during

14. **anti**
    a. for   b. hatred   c. against   d. other

15. **audi**
    a. hear   b. car   c. pain   d. ache

16. **auto**
    a. type of car   b. self   c. highway   d. self

17. **bene**
    a. beginning   b. sincere   c. harmful   d. good

18. **bi**
    a. two   b. division   c. against   d. many

19. **bio**
    a. story   b. scene   c. life   d. book

20. **cent**
    a. money   b. sensation   c.one hundred   d. contest

21. **chron**
    a. time   b. color   c. watch   d. circle

22. **cogn**
    a. live   b. know   c. read   d. memory

23. **cycl**
    a. circle   b. machine   c. cyclone   d. series

24. **dec**
    a. card game   b. platform   c. ten   d. series

25. **demos**
    a. waste   b. clouds   c. curve   d. people

26. **dia**
     a. through   b. next to   c. solid   d. on top of

27. **patri**
     a. father   b. warning   c. speech   d. speak

28. **peri**
     a. to feel   b. around   c. swing   d. inside

29. **phil**
     a. show   b. love   c. father   d. sight

30. **phobia**
     a. light   b. fear   c. power   d. hateful

31. **phon**
     a. near   b. city   c. to know   d. sound

32. **poly**
     a. many   b. few   c. oil   d. city

33. **dis**
     a. bad   b. not   c. argue   d. outside

34. **ex**
     a. different   b. beyond   c. out   d. around

35. **fin**
     a. steady   b. end   c. free   d. fix

36. **graph**
     a. comical   b. write   c. picture   d. photograph

37. **grat**
     a. please, thank   b. letter   c. note   d. grated

38. **greg**
     a. heavy   b. different   c. herd   d. not know

39. **hyper**
    a. sleep   b. know   c. cluster   d. over, above

40. **hypo**
    a. young   b. under, below   c. water   d. blood

41. **hydro**
    a. health   b. harmony   c. sacred   d. water

42. **lav**
    a. praise   b. extend   c. free   d. wash

43. **mal**
    a. bad   b. content   c. place   d. light

44. **micro**
    a. star   b. middle   c. small   d. huge

45. **migr**
    a. break   b. move   c. spark   d. place

46. **mis**
    a. wrong   b. first   c. beyond   d. into

47. **neo**
    a. old   b. new   c. antique   d. below

48. **omni**
    a. over   b. equal   c. forever   d. all

49. **pac**
    a. please, peace   b. bread   c. equal   d. wealth

50. **para**
    a. middle   b. beyond   c. alongside   d. parents

Writing Connection

You have been given a two-week, round trip airfare with hotel accommodations to a country of your choice. Write a 175-200 word paragraph explaining why you chose that country and what you hope to do and see while you are there. In your paragraph include 4 words using "con", 2 words using "peri", 3 words using "pre", and 3 words using "mis".

Chapter Summary

An extensive and expanding vocabulary will not only reflect your status in life but will also allow you to understand challenging thoughts and ideas. Increasing both the expressive and receptive vocabularies need to be emphasized. The expressive words are used to "express" ourselves in speaking and writing. We recommend students learn the Big 205 which will increase the expressive vocabulary. Receptive vocabulary is equally important. These are the words we "receive" when we read and listen. Vocabulary in context is a useful technique to learn word meanings. There are four that should be employed while "receiving information." These techniques involve finding clues of the definition of words through examining: synonyms, antonyms, examples and experience or using your general sense from the sentence(s) or paragraph of which the word appears.

Reading usually precedes writing and the impulse to write is almost always fired by reading. Reading, the love of reading, is what makes you dream of becoming a writer.
Susan Sontag

Index Strategy

""The beginning of wisdom is to call things by their right name."
Confucius

Class: All classes with assigned textbooks

Goal: To identify and learn all the terminology in the chapter

Materials Needed: Textbook, paper, index cards, colored pen or pencil

Individual or group: Individual

Lesson Duration: 45-60

Finished Product to be graded: List of words or index cards with meaning

Why do I need to learn this?

Preparing for a test can be difficult when you are uncertain which terms, names, events, and concepts are really important. This is especially true when preparing for multiple choice tests. The "Index Strategy" will help you solve that difficulty.

Procedure

1. On a piece of paper or notebook write down the page numbers from the textbook you are required to read for the upcoming test. Then go to the index.

2. With a colored pen or pencil mark every word in the index that is on the pages for your test.

3. Now you have identified all the words that might be on the test and also the page number where it appears.

4. Go to each page where the word appears and read about the word in context. Make a list of these words or put them on cards. Use the list and/or the cards for your review sessions.

How many words do you think you know?

Final Thoughts

You have to know at least 5 terms for every multiple-choice question - one term in the question stem and four terms in the four possible answers. Besides learning the meaning of the term, you will also be reading about it in the context of the chapter.

3

Fun Time with Words

"Trust yourself, you know more than you think you do."

Ben Franklin

We want you to enjoy this chapter, so just read this chapter for fun! There are no assignments or homework for you to do. In Chapter 2 we wrote that people with good vocabularies are good readers and writers and people who are good readers and writers have good vocabularies. We hope this chapter makes you more word-conscious and that you start using the new vocabulary words.

People with big vocabularies sound smart.

In this chapter you will read about:

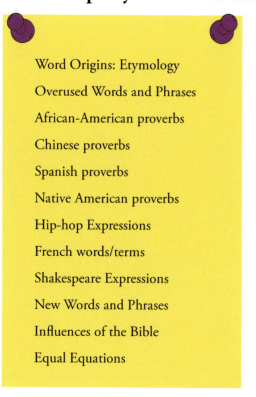

Word Origins: Etymology

Overused Words and Phrases

African-American proverbs

Chinese proverbs

Spanish proverbs

Native American proverbs

Hip-hop Expressions

French words/terms

Shakespeare Expressions

New Words and Phrases

Influences of the Bible

Equal Equations

CHALLENGE 1
Becoming a wordsmith

What is a wordsmith? Why should I want to become a wordsmith?

A wordsmith is someone who loves words and uses them skillfully. Writers and speakers want to be experts with words. One trait common with wordsmiths is their desire to add new words.

We hope you will enjoy this chapter. It has many entertaining facts and stories about the English language. Although there are no exercises at the end of the chapter, your instructor may have some creative activities such as using some of the words and phrases in writing a story, poem, or song.

You will hear the word wordsmith used a lot in college. Can you use it in a sentence?

Before you begin this chapter, try to guess how many words are in the English language?

It is difficult to give a sensible answer to this question because 1.) Some lexicographers count a word such as hope as one word while others count it as several words (*hope, hopeful, hoping, and hopeful.*) 2.) Do you count words such as sushi and tiramisu - because they come from other languages? To make everything simple and to give you an answer - English has about one million words!

Here are some more facts about English.

👉 English is spoken by one out of every six people in the world.

👉 Sixty-percent of all students studying a foreign language study English.

👉 English is the language used worldwide for air traffic control.

College students—now's your chance to become a wordsmith!

Etymology is the study of how words originated. Some of the words and phrases we use have very amusing stories or histories.

Word origins

How did *"Bringing home the bacon"* originate?
A long time ago at county fairs, a common event was to grease a pig and let him loose among several blindfolded contestants. The man who was

Just think of word origins as an interesting "oh my gosh" history lesson.

able to catch the greased pig could keep it, and that is how the saying, *"bring home the bacon"* came to be.

What does it mean to say someone has *"cold feet?"*
Soldiers often had frozen feet until the early 1900's. Because of this condition, they could only walk very slowly or timidly into battle. So, people who cannot do this quickly are said to have *"cold feet."*

Why do we say *"He drinks like a fish?"*
Almost always fish swim about with their mouths open, and we assume they are drinking water all the time. We say the same thing about someone who drinks too much.

Where did we get the expression *"Feather in his cap?"*
Every time a Native American killed an enemy, he added a feather to his headgear.

What does it mean to be *"fit as a fiddle?"*
Years ago when fiddlers played for dances, they could play for hours and hours without ever getting tired.

Why does being *"happy as a clam"* mean that someone is extremely happy?
Clams are an animal that are usually alone except at high tide when they are with other clams. Then we assume they are very happy.

Why do we say a haughty (overly proud, arrogant) person is on *"his/her high horse?"* Horsemen have a reputation for imagining they are superior to those on the ground. If he is on a high horse, he thinks she is even more superior.

What does the expression *"He has the inside track"* mean?
In horseracing the horse on the inside track is in a better position because there is less distance to cover.

Why does *"We're in the same boat"* mean we are all equal? If a ship is wrecked, everyone from first class to steerage shares a common goal - to get to safety.

How did the flower *"lavender"* get its name? A long time ago a laundress would place a sprig of lavender in the freshly cleaned clothing and bedding to give it a lovely scent.

What does *"Make the bed"* refer to?
Today we use the term *"make the bed"* when we actually "fix or do the bed." In olden days beds were often made each night because every night beds were made from straw and had to be brought into the house.

Why do we say something is *"As easy as pie?"*
Actually, the expression is *"as easy as eating pie"* and eating a pie is usually an enjoyable thing do to.

Where did the word *"muscle"* originate?
Muscle comes from the Latin musculus which means *"little mouse."* The early Romans thought that if you move your muscles in your upper arm it looks as though there is a little mouse running around inside your arm.

Who is credited with the word *"sandwich?"*
In the mid-1759s John Montague, the Earl of Sandwich loved playing cards. He never like to take the time away from his card game to eat so he put the meat between two slices of bread which enabled him to eat while continuing his card game.

Why does the expression *"Throw in the Sponge"* mean that a person realizes she/she is defeated?
Long ago during the boxing match, a trainer would throw in the sponge he used to wipe the boxer's face into the ring. This meant to everyone that the boxer could not continue and admit defeat. Today, instead of throwing in a sponge, a trainer will throw in a towel.

Why is the term *"upper crust"* used to describe people of high society? The *"upper"* or top part of the crust won bread is considered the best part and most people thought high society was the best or the "upper crust."

Why do we call someone who is unsociable at a party a *"wet blanket?"*
A "wet blanket" is used to smother a fire and a person who is lifeless or dull at a party will have the same effect as a *"wet blanket."*

Why do we call some teeth *"wisdom teeth?"*
People usually cut these teeth during the *"age of wisdom."* Some people, however, never cut their wisdom teeth!

How did *"Good Friday"* come to be?
Good Friday comes from *"God's Friday"* since Christ was crucified on that day.

What is the meaning of *"Goodbye?"*
This is a shortened version of *"God be with you."*

Where did *"varsity"* come from?
"Varsity" is the shortened word for *"university."*

Overused words

Some words and phrases are overused and tired! Although the English language has over one million words, most people never use more than 10,000. Notice if you use the following words and terms too often and, if you do, try to replace them with different words. Use your thesaurus and dictionary in your search.

Overused, tired words
Find at least two synonyms for each overused word:

very	great	amazing
wonderful	awesome	absolutely
ridiculous	like	terrible
nice	unbelievable	seriously
basically	bad	actually
literally	honestly	totally
good	whatever	

Overused, tired phrases
Select different words that mean the same as the phrases

Effort matters more than intellect.
                    Unknown

At some point in time	NO kidding	For the most part
By the same token	You guys	Larger than life
Should I tell you	It's not rocket science.	Not my thing
Sure thing	No problem	You don't know the half of it.
	I could care less.	

Proverbs

What are proverbs?

Proverbs are short, popular, simple sayings that express a common idea. Each culture has its own proverbs. The Bible contains many proverbs, many of which are found in the Book of Proverbs. You may want to ask some friends or classmates from other cultures the proverbs they heard from their parents and grandparents.

 ## African-American Proverbs

Smooth seas do not make skillful sailors.

Do not look where you fell, but where you slipped.

Only a fool tests the water with both feet.

Don't judge any man until you have walked two moons in his moccasins.

To stay a long time in the water does not make you clean.

Tell me whom you love and I'll tell you who you are.

Instruction in youth is like engraving in stone.

The orphan does not rejoice after a heavy breakfast.

If one is roasting two potatoes, one of them is bound to get charred.

People know each other better on a journey.

A fool has to say something. A wise person has something to say.

Chinese Proverbs

Teachers open the door but you must walk through it yourself.

If you are patient in one moment of anger, you will escape a hundred

days of sorrow.

A clear conscience never fears midnight knocking.

A dog won't forsake his master because of poverty.

A son never deserts his mother for her homely appearance.

When planning for a year, plant corn. When planning for a decade, plant

trees. When planning for a lifetime, train and educate people.

Pick the flower when it is ready to be picked.

Everything has its beauty but not everyone sees it.

The superior man is modest in his speech, but excels in his actions.

If a son is uneducated, his father is to blame.

To know the road ahead, ask those coming back.

Spanish Proverbs

Who loves me, loves my dog.

He who walks with the lame learns how to limp.

War is sweet to those who have never fought.

A friend to everybody and nobody is the same thing.

For a good appetite there is no hard bread.

Imitation is the sincerely form of flattery.

In the land of the blind, the one-eyed is king.

While the fool is thinking, the wise man makes his fortune.

The madman who knows how to keep silent is held to be sane.

Just because my path is different doesn't mean I'm lost.

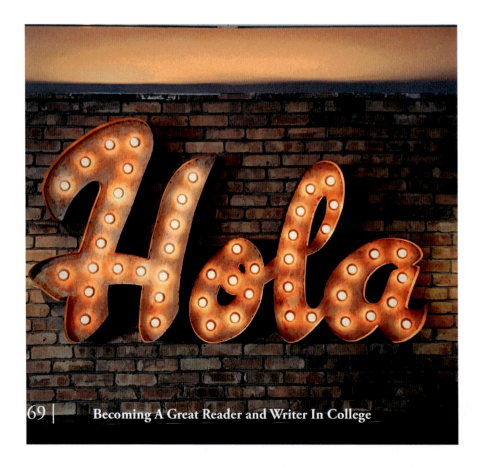

Native-American Proverbs

It is easy to be brave from a distance.

Nobody gets out of the bed to sleep on the floor.

The lazy ox drinks dirty water.

We will be known forever by the tracks we leave.

Those that lie down with dogs, get up with fleas.

One finger cannot lift a pebble.

Seek wisdom, not knowledge, knowledge is of the past, wisdom is of the future.

The frog does not drink up the pond in which he lives.

Don't let yesterday use up too much of today.

Day and night cannot dwell together.

Hip-Hop Expressions

What are hip-hop expressions?

Language is constantly changing, especially the English language. Hip hop which used to be found only in music and dance is now a widely form of communication used by young people all over the world. Some of it reflects the ill-feelings and displeasure toward the mainstream culture and society.

Aight	verb	the contraction for all right
All that	noun	something that is nice and pleasant to you or others
Bail out	verb	to run away
Bulla	noun	someone with a lot of money
Beantown	noun	Boston
Beat juice	verb	to drink alcohol
Benjamins	noun	twenty dollar bills
Billie	noun	money from a dollar bill
Boo-ya	adjective	totally, incredibly fine
Break bread	verb	share money or information
Brother	noun	black male, man of the same group, friend
C-town	noun	Cleveland, Ohio
Chi-town	noun	Chicago, Illinois

These expressions are 'old school'. Do you know some current expressions?

Chocolate City	noun	Washington, DC
D-town	noun	Dallas, Texas or Detroit, Michigan
Flow	noun	money, cash
Freak	verb	to behave in a provocative way
Ghetto sled	noun	very old American car usually covered with house paint but in excellent condition inside and out
Hella	noun	a hell of a lot
Hoopie	verb	an old car in bad shape
Jesus juice	noun	cheap wine mixed with coke
Ride	noun	your car
Shool	adjective	to teach
Straight	verb	OK, good
Word	noun	honest truth

French Word/Terms

Why are French words so popular?
Many people think the French language is beautiful because of the accent and its melody. It sounds cultured and upper class! Maybe it's popular because people associate France and Paris with art, cuisine, and the luxurious brands of clothing, accessories and perfumes. Until 1956 it was the language of the elite and used to be the international language of diplomacy and philosophical discussion. Here are some commonly used French expressions.

A la carte	food from a menu that is priced separately
A la mode	served with ice cream
Au pair	young foreigner who does domestic work and child care
Au gratin	anything that is grated, usually cheese
Au jus	with juice from meat
Avant garde	offbeat, advanced guard
Baguette	small, thin narrow loaf of bread
Belle	popular and attractive woman
Blasé	unconcerned, apathetic
Bon vivant	one who likes to live well, a gourmet
Bon voyage	good journey
Boulevard	a broad often landscaped thoroughfare
Cache	a collection of items usually stored in a hidden place
Café au lait	coffee with milk or cream
Canape	small decorative food held in one hand and eaten in one bite
C'est la vie	That's life!

Chauffer	a driver
Chignon	a hair style worn with a roll at the back of the neck
Cliché	a trite, overused phrase
Clique	exclusive group of friends
Concierage	receptionist at a hotel
Crepes	small pancakes filled with fruit, meats, or vegetables
Croissant	crescent shaped roll with flaky dough
Décor	the design, layout, and furnishings of a room
Eau de cologne	cologne water
Éclair	a chocolate frosted oblong pastry
Entrée	main course
Flambe	food served with a flaming liquor
Faux pas	a mistake
Mousse	a light, spongy food made with cream or gelatin or a hair dressing
Petit fous	a small cake cut from pound or sponge cake and frosted
Plat du jour	special of the day
Omelette	omelet

Shakespearean Expressions

Common Shakespearean expressions
If you want to impress your friends and teachers, try to use some of these in your everyday conversations!

"As luck would have it"	Merry Wives of Windsor
"As merry as the day is long"	Much Ado About Nothing
"Bated breath"	Merchant of Venice
"Be all and the end all."	MacBeth
"Brave New World"	The Tempest
"Break the Ice"	Taming of the Shrew
"Brevity is the soul of wit."	Hamlet
"But love is blind and lovers cannot see."	The Merchant of Venic
"Cowards die many times before their death. The valiant never taste of death but once."	Julius Caesar
"Conscience does make cowards of us all."	Hamlet
"Dead as a doornail"	Henry V, Part 2
"A dish fit for the gods"	Julius Caesar
"Eaten me out of house and home."	Julius Caesar
"Forever and a day"	As You Like It
"For goodness sake"	Henry VIII
"Foregone conclusion"	Othello
"Give the devil his due."	Henry IV, Part 1
"Heart of Gold"	Henry V

"In my heart of hearts"   Hamlet

"In my mind's eye"   Hamlet

"Love is Blind."   Merchant of Venice

"Neither a borrower or lender be"   Hamlet

"Refuse to budge an inch"   The Taming of the Shrew

"To be or not to be, that is the   Hamlet
question."

"Wear my heart on my sleeve"   Othello

"Wild goose chase"   Romeo and Juliet

New Words and Phrases

Some of these words can be found in dictionaries while others may never get there!

Boat anchor   useless computer

Cement city   cemetery

Couch commerce   buying goods online from home

Cyberloaf   spending time on the internet at
                           work doing personal things

Daycation   a trip or short vacation lasting only
                           one day

Doubleday   a holiday celebrated for 48 hours or
                           2 days

Dramedy   a mix of drama and comedy

Earworm   a tune that keeps repeating itself
                           over and over in our heads

Fallophobic   a person with an extreme fear of
                           fallowing

Flexitarian   a vegetarian who sometimes eats
                           meat or fish

Flightmare   a blend of flight and nightmares -
                           an unpleasant flight experience

Floordrobe   a blend of floor and wardrobe - a
                           pile of clothes dropped on the floor

Frenemy   an enemy who pretends to be
                           your friend

Gran-lit   books that older people like

Graycation   going on a vacation with
                           grandparents who will pay
                           all expenses

Hamdog	combination of hamburger and hotdog
Informania	constantly checking and answering emails and texts
NEET	no experience, education, or training
Password fatigue	being tired of having to remember large number of passwords
Pursable	able to carry in a purse
Screeager	a young person or teenager who spends a lot of time in front of the computer screen
Trashion	a blend of trash and fashion—fashionable clothing made from old, used and recycled things
Shaket	a light jacket similar to a shirt

Influences of The Bible

The following common phrases have Biblical origins.
Read them and then look them up in the Bible. Make sure you understand their meaning.

A drop in the bucket	Isaiah 40:15
A house divided cannot stand.	Matthew 12:25
A scapegoat	Leviticus 16:9-10
An eye for an eye, a tooth for a tooth.	Matthew 5:38
At one's wits' end	Psalms 107:27
Can a leopard change its spots?	Jeremiah 13:23
Cast pearls before swine.	Matthew 7:6
Cast the first stone.	John 8:7
Go the extra mile.	Matthew 5:41
Rise and shine	Isaiah 60:1
There's nothing new under the sun.	Ecclesiastes 1:9
To everything there is a season.	Ecclesiastes 3:1

How many of these expressions do you use?

Equal Equations

"A deal is a deal"

"It is what it is"

"Less is more, more is better."

"The past is the past."

"The law is the law."

"Right is right, wrong is wrong."

Chapter Summary

We hope you enjoyed this chapter and that you will become more interested in words. Remember to use your new words in speaking and writing. Notice the words that accomplished, educated people use. Isn't it great becoming a wordsmith?

ABLE Strategy
"Always Be A Little Early"

"Better three hours too soon than a minute too late."

William Shakespeare

Course: All courses

Goal: To always be on time

Material Needed: Planner or small notebook for a daily "To-Do List" watch or cell phone

Individual or group: Individual

Lesson Duration: Ongoing

Finished Product to be graded: Planner or small notebooks that has completed events/appointments

---

Why do I need to learn this?

The "Be Early Principle" is to always be a little early or at least "on time." This is an easy habit to acquire and one that will serve you in your daily and professional life. In fact, it could make the difference being successful and very successful. Being a little early shows respect, interest, and reliability. Instructors appreciate students who arrive early; they begin to have negative feelings toward those students who continually show up late.

Procedure

1. Record all due dates for assignments, projects, meetings, and appointments in a monthly planner or in your cell phone.

2. Allow extra time to complete assignments, to prepare for exams, and to get to class.

3. Allow extra time for traveling by car and for parking. The additional time will give you the flexibility for the "unexpected."

4. Always take a book or something to study as you wait for class or appointments.

5. Make preparations the night before. Select your clothing, pack your backpack, and have your keys in a visible place.

Final Thoughts

People always notice those who are early. The ones who are always on time give the impression that they are dependable. If you are five minutes early to a class, you can skim through your textbook and get ready for the class.

4

Advancing to College Reading: The Main Idea

"Between the pages of a book is a wonderful place to be."

Anonymous

April 7, 2016

Dear Diary,

I am so upset!! I just feel like crying. Today I got back the history test and got another C. I don't understand why I got such a low grade when I studied for hours. I read all the chapters and studied my notes. I thought I knew everything. I will go to see Dr. Brett tomorrow and ask to see my test to figure out why I did so poorly.

Samantha

April 8, 2016

Dear Diary,

I saw Dr. Brett today and we went over my history test. I got most of the detail questions right but

Dr. Brett said I missed the main idea type questions. She said by looking at my wrong answers, she

could tell I didn't understand "the big picture". For example, I missed a question that asked the

purpose of the Lewis and Clark Expedition. I didn't know that but I memorized so many details.....I

even knew how many people went on the Lewis and Clark Expedition and where they were from!

She told me about five times that understanding the main idea is the most important task when

trying to learn something. She suggested that I read one paragraph at a time, stop and write the

main idea in the margin. She also said I should find the main idea first because when the main

idea is known, the details fall naturally in place. I feel a little better today. I know now I will

make sure I always learn the main idea first, and then the details. By the way, Diary, I always

feel better after writing to you.

Samantha

Developing reading competency is progressive - no one becomes a skillful reader overnight - it may take years to become the reader you know you can become. Reading skills are developed sequentially - first sounds, matching sounds with letters, fluency, comprehension, and critical thinking. When one part or stage in the reading breaks down or is weakened, reading problems occur and the whole reading process is impaired.

In this chapter you will read about:

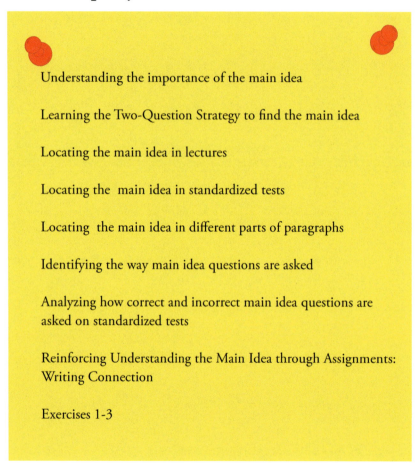

Understanding the importance of the main idea

Learning the Two-Question Strategy to find the main idea

Locating the main idea in lectures

Locating the main idea in standardized tests

Locating the main idea in different parts of paragraphs

Identifying the way main idea questions are asked

Analyzing how correct and incorrect main idea questions are asked on standardized tests

Reinforcing Understanding the Main Idea through Assignments: Writing Connection

Exercises 1-3

CHALLENGE 1
Learning all about the main idea

Introduction: Main Idea

The Main Idea is the most important point the author is trying to make and it's the most important key to good comprehension.

Writing Connection

Respond: Choose a textbook chapter you are currently reading. What is the main idea of the assigned chapter? Write it below. Describe to the class how you determined the main idea.

_____

_____

_____

_____

After reading this chapter, revisit your answer. Do you still agree that your main idea is correct? If not, rewrite the main idea.

Although most people associate the main idea with reading, we answer main idea questions all the time. In conversation, a friend may ask,

	Answer is a main idea
"What was that new movie about?"	"The movie was about how a divorced couple got together again after twenty years."
"What happened in class today?"	"Today we reviewed mitosis and then we started meiosis."
"Why do you want to go to graduate school?"	"I want another degree."

Understanding the importance of the topic

Determining the topic is the first step to recognizing the main idea.

The topic is the subject of a paragraph, section, or chapter that is expressed in a word or phrase. You can determine the topic sentence by asking, "Who or what is the paragraph or passage about?" Let's take the topic, Disney World, which is a broad, one word topic. The statement, "Disney World, is a great amusement park for families" is a main idea statement under which more information and details will be added. Textbooks that have headings and titles from the reading selections usually contain the subject, which gives the reader a "head start" to finding the main idea.

Understanding the importance of the topic sentence

The topic sentence is usually the first sentence in a paragraph although it can also be in the middle or the end. This is the sentence that states the main idea or main points of a paragraph.

Understanding the importance of the main idea

Identifying the main idea is the most important point the author is making in the paragraph. It is usually found in the topic sentence. Some experts say it is "essential to understanding" written material because finding the main idea is almost always the first step in comprehending. It's important to know that a main idea can be found in a paragraph, a section, or a chapter.

We usually associate the main idea with reading material, but a main idea is also found in lectures, power point presentations, standardized tests, and even visual material such as graphs, charts, illustrations, and diagrams. We even use the main idea in our interactions with others. For example, if your friend asks, "What is your school like?" you would simply give a main idea answer such as, "My school has about 5,000

The topic sentence consists of the topic, the overall happening of the topic and some details. Most of the time the main idea is in the topic sentence but it is NOT necessarily the entire topic sentence. The main idea is usually the "what" and the overall what is happening with NO details.

students and we won the state championship in football this year." Notice that only the main idea about the school was given. If, however, your friend wanted more information, you would follow that general statement of the main idea with lots of details that support it.

The main idea is also known as the major point, the controlling idea, thesis, central thought, or the gist. The main idea is like an open umbrella because all the details are brought together and fit under it. The details develop, expand, and add more information about the main idea.

Key points to remember are:
1. The most important reading skill is determining the main idea of a paragraph, section, or chapter.

2. Comprehension is increased when the main idea is known.

Learning the Two-Question Strategy to find the main idea of a passage

To determine the main idea of any discourse, use this simple *Two-Question Strategy:*

To determine the main idea of material, in a text, ask:
1. Who or what is the paragraph or passage about?

2. What is happening with that who or what?

Finding the main idea from reading material and standardized tests can be found by using the ***Two-Question Strategy.*** Usually finding the main idea of passages from textbooks is a straightforward activity because the title of the chapter, headings, and subheadings usually contain the topic. Knowing the topic is the answer to the first question in the ***Two-Question Strategy.*** The answer to the second question together with the topic will be the main idea.

Sometimes finding the main idea can be a more challenging task as in these examples:

👉 Paragraphs and sections which have implied main ideas rather than those that have directly stated main ideas, and

Paragraphs and sections which do not have titles, topic sentences, and headings.

These situations require the reader to continue to use the ***Two-Question Strategy*** and also to use inference and reasoning skills. This means that the reader must read and assimilate all the information to determine the correct topic and main idea.

Example 1 is a paragraph with a directly stated main idea.

A new study supports the idea that yawning is beneficial to the brain. Most people try to stifle yawns, especially in the presence of their teacher or boss. They think yawning shows rudeness or boredom. However, research explains that yawning helps cool down our brain and even helps it to work better. Researchers compared the brain to show that the brain, like the computer, functions better when it is cool. When you have a "cool brain" you are more likely to absorb information. So, the next time you feel like yawning, don't stifle it…it's good for your brain!

	This is the topic
Who or what is this passage about?	***Yawning***
	This is the main idea. Notice it is also a topic sentence.
What is happening with the who or what?	***New research shows yawning is beneficial to the brain.***

Example 2 also features a paragraph with a stated main idea. Read and apply the ***Two-Question Strategy.***

The English language has many expressions that have been handed down over the years. Since the 1500's, most people use these without knowing their origins or that the origin can be amusing. "Upper crust," considered the best part of the bread was the top or crust, and it was always given to visitors while the rest of the family got the burnt bottom or middle. If a man "brought home the bacon," he was probably richer than most, so he hung the bacon in a prominent place for all to see. When visitors came, a piece of the bacon was cut off and everyone sat around and "chewed the fat." The saying, "dirt poor" referred to poor people who could not afford flooring material such as slate. Their floors were hard, packed dirt.

Who or what is this passage about? _____

What is happening with the who or what? _____

Below is a sample chapter section. Read the section and determine the main idea.

Checks and Balances

The United States government is set up with three branches that check and balance each other. The architects of our constitution created a fundamental principle underlying the power and tension of the federal government. The objective was that the founding fathers did not want any of the three branches to be too powerful. So, for almost every power each branch was given, equal power of control was given to the other two branches. Therefore, each branch can check the power of the other.

The President of the United States has executive powers. The President is the chief executive in the country. He or she approves or vetoes federal bills, carries out federal laws, appoints judges and other high officials, makes foreign treaties, can grant pardons and reprieves to federal treaties. He is also the commander-in-chief of the armed forces. To make sure the President's office does not get too powerful, Congress can override vetoes by two-thirds vote, the senate can refuse to confirm appointments or ratify treaties. Other checks placed on the executive office is that Congress can impeach and remove the President, declare war and the Supreme Court can declare executive acts unconstitutional.

Analyze this article for the main idea. Is there an overall main idea and then a main idea for each section? Is the main idea located in the topic sentence?

The Senate and the House of Representatives also have checks. The President can veto federal bills passed by the house and senate, the Supreme Court can rule that laws passed by the legislature are unconstitutional, and both houses of Congress must vote to pass laws.

Checks on the Judicial branch include the requirement of a two-thirds majority vote by both houses to overturn a judicial decision. Congress can impeach or remove a federal judge and the President appoints judges who must be confirmed by the senate.

What is the main idea of this chapter section?

_____

_____

_____

_____

_____

Answer
What is the topic/subject?
Checks and balance in the three branches of the U.S. government.

What is the text saying about checks and balances?
The United States government has a method for checking each of its three branches to make sure no branch becomes more powerful than the other.

Main Idea
The United States government has a method of checking each of its three branches to make sure no branch becomes too powerful.

Analysis
Again, the topic is obvious because it is directly written on the heading. However, the reader needs to ask, "so what is the author saying about checks and balances?" In this case, the main idea was written using terms and phrases to define checks and balances in order to ensure that the main idea statement is "crystal clear."

Locating the main ideas in lectures

Lectures can range from simple oral presentations to more formal oral presentations supported by power point slides. Finding the main idea from lectures is one of the first tasks you should do to become an effective note taker. This is only the beginning of the learning task, but it is very important. Lectures are a continuous story of information---each lecture builds from previous lectures. Use the ***Two-Question Strategy*** to find the main idea.

Who or What is the topic/subject of the speech or lecture?
What is being said about the Who or What?

Can you see that we're really asking the same question, but now targeting lectures?

Below is a mini lecture. Read the lecture and then write the main idea using the Two-Question Strategy.

Flight

While waiting for the flight at the airport, one of the many thoughts that may come to mind is: How do planes fly? The question may appear complex, but the answer is rather simple. Planes require two things to fly: thrust and lift. Thrust is the forward motion provided by a propeller or jet engine of a plane. Planes also fly using lift. Danielle Bernoulli explained lift in his principle, Bernoulli's Principle, and today we will go further than just discussing the principle: we will create lift! We will make a piece of paper fly! But, before we do that, let's examine his principle.

Bernoulli's principle describes that if air speeds up and pressure is low, then the wing of the plane generates lift. Pressure is defined as a force over an area. Remember an airplane wing has a special shape called an airfoil. This means that the wing budges more on top than on the bottom. When the air meets the wing, it splits into two streams, top and bottom. The air passing over the top has to travel farther than the air going underneath. Since the air above the wing has less pressure than area below, the wing creates lift. In other words, air moving over a curved surface top of the wing has more distance to travel than the air under the wing. Since the air on top of the wing is moving faster than the air below, a lower pressure above the wing is created. This causes a force to exert under the wing lifting the wing upward. If the air moves fast enough over the surface of the wing, the lift force can overcome gravity. The speed is generated by thrust. In our next session we will discuss the other two forces, gravity and thrust, in terms of how they affect flight. We'll discuss Newton's Law and how it explains flight.

Analyze the lecture in terms of main ideas for each paragraph and where they are located.

Now let's give flight to a piece of paper. Cut a two-inch wide strip of newspaper or notebook paper. The strip should be about ten inches long. Hold one end of the strip just below the mouth. Let the rest of the strip hang freely. Blow hard over the top of the strip and watch what happens.

What is the main idea of this chapter section?

_____

_____

_____

Answer
What is the topic/subject?
<u>Flight</u>

What is the text saying about checks and balances?
<u>Thrust and lift cause airplanes to fly.</u>

Main Idea
<u>Flight is caused by thrust and lift.</u>

Analysis
<u>The first part of the lecture is very straight forward: the topic is flight. The professor will give the topic throughout the lecture. However, the second part of the main idea is spread throughout the lecture. So what is the professor saying about flight? Flight happens by thrust and lift. Remember, the main idea does not include details. Therefore any response including details of how thrust or lift works to lift an airplane is not needed. In fact, that is not the main idea. It is a detail and will probably be the correct answer for a supporting detail question and not a main idea question.</u>

Locating the main idea in standarized tests

Standardized tests usually include main idea questions. The test will have main idea questions about individual paragraphs or an entire passage. Main ideas may either be stated or implied.

Stated and Implied Main Ideas on Standardized Tests

The computer in my high school class recently started acting up. After watching me struggle with it, one of my students came over and took over. "Your hard drive crashed." I called the computer services office and explained, "My computer is down. The hard drive crashed." How do you know that's the problem?" "A student told me," I answered. "We'll send someone right away."

The implied main idea is that people assume that "young people" know more about computers than older people.

A stated main idea means that the main idea is stated in a topic sentence. Remember, a topic sentence is the sentence in the paragraphs that states the topic of the paragraph and indicates the general matter to be discussed in the paragraph.

Often the topic sentence is in the first sentence although it can appear anywhere in the paragraph. **Some important things to remember are that the main idea comes from the topic sentence, but often the topic sentence has more information than is needed for the main idea. An implied main idea is not directly stated. It must be inferred and often the reader must use background information.**

When you are asked to choose the correct main idea on a standardized test, be aware that the correct choice may be rephrased - it may not have the same wording but the rephrased choice has the same meaning.

If you use the ***Two-Question Strategy*** you will undoubtedly choose the correct topic and main idea because the main idea only answers the two questions. On standardized tests, choices for main idea questions often have two answers which both seem correct. Any information that includes details, such as when, where and why should not be considered part of the main idea. You must be able to make the fine distinction between topic sentences and main idea statements because on most tests, they both appear as a choice.

Answering main idea questions from paragraphs or passages without stated topic sentences requires reasoning and inference because the main idea must be implied. Using the Two-Question Strategy helps you select the correct answer on standardized tests. Answering implied main idea questions will be discussed fully in chapter 4, Understanding Implied Main Ideas.

Finding the main idea in different parts of paragraphs

Now let's examine four different samples featuring the main idea in the beginning, middle, end, and split with one section in the beginning and the other at the end.

Main Idea in the beginning

Topic Sentence
Details
Details

I had excellent listening, speaking, and memory skills when I worked as a waiter. On that first day as a server, my listening skills were very sharp! I was able to remember every customer's special request and especially those customers who wanted substitutions and all the details about how the food was prepared. I consistently remembered to address my customers with the upmost respect and used the terms "sir" and "ma'am." I worked ten hours as a waiter that day and left very pleased with my performance.

Analysis
Who or what is the paragraph about?
<u>My first day at work.</u>

What about that who or what?
<u>I was confident that I had all the necessary skills.</u>

Main Idea
<u>I was confident on my first day of work.</u>
Notice that the main idea came from the topic sentence, but is not the topic sentence. Also notice that topic sentence gave more information than needed for the main idea.

Analyze this

Main Idea at the middle

Details
Details
Topic Sentence
Details
Details

Many may think that the calmness of the sea is boring. Others think that the gentle rocking of the boat with the quiet splash against the bow serves no purpose for as a favorite get away. **(However, I think that the calm seas is the best get away that anyone can encounter.)** It offers piece of mind from the everyday hustle and bustle. But more importantly, it allows you to get in touch with your inner feelings and experience a sense of calmness. Once that happens, the pressures of life are noticeably reduced.

Analysis
Who or what is the paragraph about?
Calm Seas.

What about that who or what?
Best get away.

Main Idea
Calm Seas is the best get away.
Notice that the main idea came from the topic sentence, but is not the first sentence. Also notice that the topic sentence gave more information than needed for the main idea.

Analyze this

97 | **Becoming A Great Reader and Writer In College**

Main Idea at the end

Details
Details
Topic Sentence

Analyze this

It was raining hard on the interstate as I made the one hour drive home. The traffic moved at a snail's pace forcing me to stop and go the entire trip. The right side of the interstate was bordered with automobiles that were in accidents or with drivers who had given up driving in the slow track during the heavy rain. But, the worst part of the trip home was the overworked and tired drivers who blew their horns every minute. My trip home on the interstate was one of the worst because the weather was bad, the traffic moved slowly, and the drivers were angry.

Analysis

Who or what is the paragraph about? <u>My trip home on the interstate.</u>
What about that who or what? <u>One of the worst.</u>

Main Idea

<u>My trip home on the interstate was one of the worst.</u>
Again, details from the topic sentence are not used for the main idea.

Main Idea at the beginning and end

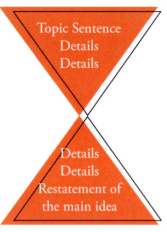

Topic Sentence
Details
Details

Details
Details
Restatement of
the main idea

Ski boarding is a winter sport that combines, skating, and skiing. Ski boarding was invented by skaters who desire the same skate-like ease on the snowy slopes that they get on skates. Ski boards stop and turn just like skates. The balance and upright position used on ski boards is the same used on skates. However, the boot bindings on ski boards are like traditional skis except ski board boot bindings are attached to the board in a perpendicular fashion. The movement to negotiate down slopes or to make jumps are the same as on skis. Thus, learning to ski board means skating and skiing.

Analyze this

Analysis

Who or what is the paragraph about?
Ski boarding.

What about that who or what?
Ski boarding involves skating and skiing.

Becoming A Great Reader and Writer In College

Implied main ideas

Paragraphs that are written in the implied main idea pattern do not have a topic sentence. This pattern consist of information after information after information, that means, details, details, and details. It is this pattern that the reader must strongly rely on the Two-Question Strategy to find the main idea.

Details

Details

Details

It is important to place the dinner plate one inch form the edge of the table. If there is a pattern in the middle of the plate, make sure the pattern is right side up. Next, place the knife on the right side of the plate with the blade inward.

The knife should be next to the plate not underneath the plate. The tablespoon is placed next to the knife. Both the knife and tablespoon are one inch from the edge of the table. The fork is places on the left side of the dinner plate. The napkin is folded in half and placed next to the fork with the crease farthest away from the fork. The glass is placed directly above the knife. Now, let's eat.

Analyze this

Analysis

This is a prime example of an implied main idea. As you can see a topic sentence is absent from the paragraph. So ask yourself who or what this paragraph is about? What is happening with that who or what? Now write your main idea.

The main idea is: _____

Now check your answer:
Who or what is the paragraph about?
How to set a table.

What is happening with that who or what?
There are certain locations for the silverware, plates and glasses.

Main Idea:
The table is set with the silverware, plates and glasses in its proper place. Notice I did not give any details, simply gave the gist or main point of the paragraph.

Identifying ways main idea questions are asked

1. What is the main idea expressed in the lecture, paragraph or passage?

2. What is the central thought of the lecture, paragraph, or passage?

3. What is the controlling idea of the lecture, paragraph, or passage?

4. What is the main point of the lecture, paragraph, or passage?

5. What is the key point of the lecture, paragraph, or passage?

6. What is the chief point of the lecture, paragraph, or passage?

7. What would be a good title for this lecture, paragraph, or passage?

Analyzing how correct and incorrect main idea questions are asked on standardized tests

Passages on a standardized test usually come from textbooks, independent writers, lectures, essays, newspapers, magazines, or they are made by the text makers. The level of difficulty is usually advanced high school level and prior knowledge of the passage subject is usually not necessary. To keep the test standardized and uniform, correct options are usually worded one way and incorrect options usually fall into 6 main categories.

Correct options:

👉 A restatement or paraphrase of the main idea of a paragraph or entire passage.

👉 A statement that answers who or what and what is happening to the who or what.

Incorrect options:

☞ A statement that misrepresents information with the topic sentence, paragraph, or passage.

☞ A misrepresentation of the topic or the who or what the topic sentence, paragraph or passage. For example, the main idea offers a boat for a topic when the topic is about a plane.

☞ A correct supporting detail. For example, the main idea statement includes details from the topic sentence.

☞ A misrepresentation of what is happening with the who or what in the topic sentence, paragraph, or passage. For example, the main idea states that the plane cannot fly when the paragraph states the plane is low on fuel so the pilot is afraid to fly it.

☞ A statement that includes the correct main idea and also includes a correct detail, inference, conclusion. For example, the main idea statement includes more information than the answers of the two questions.

☞ An incomplete main idea such as stating only the who or what or only stating what is happening with that, who, or what. For example, a statement that only gives the topic.

Reinforcing understanding of the main ideas through assignments

Writing Connection

Read the details listed below. Use these details and at least two of the Big 205 words, write 1 - 2 paragraph(s). Do not use the same academic vocabulary words you used in Chapter 1 Writing Connection. Make sure you include a strong topic sentence. You do not have to use the details in the order that they are presented below. Use your personal 205 dictionary to help you.

1. driving fast/speeding sports car

2. road with turns and twists

3. upcoming 18-wheel truck

4. panic

5. obey the speed limit

6. highway patrol/police

"Write, rewrite. When not writing or rewriting, read. I know of no shortcuts."
Larry L. King

Exercise 1: Practice with Topic Sentences

Read the paragraphs and underline the topic sentence.

1. In 1924 Clarence Birdseye had a novel idea for preserving food after a trip to Newfoundland. He observed that the people left their freshly caught fish outside and then were able to cook the fish a week later. He said the frozen fish tasted as good as the fresh fish! Birdseye realized that as soon as food is harvested, slaughtered, gathered, or caught, bacteria and other microorganisms could cause spoilage.

2. Producing a television show requires the orchestration of many specialists. The producer and director create a cast of production specialists from the onset to the actual broadcast. An art director is responsible for the show's staging and scenery. A costume designer designs and creates all clothing and costumes for the entire cast. A property manager gets the necessary props such as accessories, furniture, and cars. Technology specialists advise on the type of lighting, cameras, and microphones to be used. A production manager coordinates al the specialists so that everything runs smoothly.

3. Manatees are an endangered species, but the Crystal River National Wildlife Refuge provides a warm water haven to 15-20% of the US manatee population. Although many migrate during the summer to Virginia and North Carolina, here the manatees have a safe, protected home. The Crystal River National Wildlife Refuge can only be reached via boat. Manatees are friendly and welcome visitors who want to observe or swim with them. Manatees are endangered because they are nearsighted and more often than not are injured or killed by speeding boats.

4. Fenway Park was built in 1912 and in those early days the seats were narrow with no legroom, the scoreboard was hand operated, and pitchers warmed up in clear view of the fans. There were only 36,298 seats available for night games because one bleacher section had to be covered so the sun's glare wouldn't distract the batters. Boston Red Sox fans liked and wanted to keep Fenway Park just the way it was. Getting tickets to a game is difficult because season holders rarely give up their tickets. Fenway Park, home of the Boston Red Sox baseball team, does not have the amenities that modern baseball parks have, but it definitely has charm and has earned the name, the "granddaddy of all ballparks."

5. Some interesting words scam artists use are "evergreen," which is a scam used a lot that produces lots of money and "fish". A "fish" is a potential person marked for a scheme. A "mooch list" is a list of telephone numbers for a telemarketing scheme. Scam artists specializing in deceit or graft use unusual terms or slang usually known to each other. Some other examples are "paper players" - they are card players who use marked cards. A "top world bank" is a fake bank which is meant to sound legitimate and stable, and a "rube" is a victim or target for an upcoming scheme.

6. Many factors should be considered when selecting a city to host a major sporting event. Most major cities would like to host because there is a lot of revenue generated, besides the positive portrayal of the city. Some of the criteria for finding the perfect city would be for locals to embrace the event along with city officials to provide support and organization. Weather conditions, a large number of restaurants and transportation accessibility to the city center are other considerations.

7. South Beach has a central location, many restaurants, hotels, shopping, desirable weather, stadiums, golf courses, arenas, casinos, and racetracks. An extra bonus for Miami is the number of celebrities who frequent popular night spots all year long. There is always something to do in the areas adjacent to South Beach. It's no wonder that Miami, Florida ranks #1 as the best city to host sporting events.

8. An interesting feature of Palladian architecture is that the homes are designed so that most of the area inside the home could have views of the surrounding countryside. Today Palladian windows are used widely in the US. These wide windows have a semicircular arch overhead. Thomas Jefferson's home, Monticello, is a good example of Palladian architecture. The Rotunda at the University of Virginia is another example of classical Palladian. The most well-known house inspired by Palladian architecture

is the White House in Washington, DC. The Palladian Revival Period with excellent examples of this style is based on the Italian architect, Andres Palladio, who lived in the 16th Century.

9. The last quarter of the 19th Century in America was known as the "Age of Invention," a time when many technological advances and inventions by the "captains of industry" tremendously changed the American way of life. One notable "captain of industry" was Thomas A. Edison whose electrical invention led to dramatic changes in both industry and in the home all over the world. Edison is also known for saying that genius is "one percent inspiration and 99 percent perspiration." Another "captain of industry" was Andrew Carnegie, the steel entrepreneur who built one of the largest steel companies in the world. Carnegie was also a humanitarian and used his great wealth to establish over 2,500 libraries in the US and contributing generously to public education.

Exercise 2: Practice writing topic sentences

Read each passage and write a topic sentence in the space provided which might be in the beginning, the middle or end of the paragraph.

1. It doesn't matter what kind of notebook or journal you use for writing your private thoughts and feelings. The important thing is you will be preserving your memories, wishes, hopes, and goals. _____
_____.
Journaling will improve your writing ability as well as preserve past and present important ideas, dreams, and reflections.

2. I like seeing all the activities spread out for the entire month. A quick glance will let me know which events are the important ones because I have probably highlighted or surrounded them with fancy, colorful doodles. _____.
I like writing things down on a planner. I prefer a paper and pencil planner rather than an electronic one.

3._____
Sometimes we respond to praise by shrugging it off or saying, 'Oh, it's really nothing.' Other people will respond to a compliment by automatically returning a compliment. A few people might say, 'Do you really think so?' which subtly questions the character of the one giving the compliment.

4. Education is something that is always with you and something that is stored in your head. It will last a lifetime because it won't wear out or be stolen. It can't be destroyed or loaned to someone. Being educated leads to a lot of financial, social, and psychological opportunities. _____ _____.

5. Vegans eat a lot of beans, legumes, vegetables, and fruits. They do not eat dairy and meat products. _____ _____.
Vegans can eat tofu, peanut butter sandwiches, chips and salsa, spaghetti, and green salads. There are a lot of substitute products such as veggie burgers and non-dairy products that include cheese, milk, eggs, mayonnaise, and butter.

6. Among his many awards and titles, Lebron James has won three NBA championships, 4 NBA Most Valuable Player Awards, two Olympic gold medals. He has been selected to thirteen NBA All Star teams and is the Cleveland Cavaliers all-time leading scorer. _____ _____.
Lebron joined the Cleveland Cavaliers in 2003 and became a superstar. He joined the Miami Heat in 2010 and stayed until 2014 when he returned to the Cleveland Cavaliers. In 2018 he joined the Los Angeles Lakers!

7. It's important for college students to have a comfortable relationship with their college advisor. The college advisor should be a good listener, show a personal interest, and allow enough time to produce results. If the advisor does not have the above qualities, the student must either discuss the "lack of satisfaction" or else ask for another advisor. _____ _____.

8. College counselors urge freshmen students to join campus organizations so they can meet people with similar interests, gain experience, and improve social skills, improve a resume and to widen opportunities through networking. There are some "natural joiners" as well as "reluctant joiners." _____.

9. Traveling in the economy section for a fourteen hour flight can be an uncomfortable experience. But with the Boeing 787 Dreamliner with its bigger windows, at least six feet of vertical space, mood lighting, and not having jet lag makes me glad that I didn't spend an extra three to four thousand dollars to travel in business or first class. _____ _____.

Another reason why the Dreamliner is good for long haul flights is that the passengers don't need to use noise canceling headphones because there is less noise in the cabin. The Dreamliner holds 375 passengers, can fly nonstop for 8000 miles, and is 20% more fuel efficient.

Exercise 3: Practice finding the main idea

Read the passage. Identify the topic. Ask "What is the topic and what is being said about the topic?" - this will be the main idea.

1. Lyndon Baines Johnson, John F. Kennedy's vice president, became the president after Kennedy was assassinated in Dallas, Texas in 1963. His social agenda, "The Great Society" included the most sweeping changes in US government since Roosevelt's New Deal. Some of the legislation was The Civil Rights Act of 1964 which is considered one of the greatest antidiscrimination laws in US history, the Equal Employment Opportunity Commission, Voting Rights Act of 1965, the Economic Opportunity Act, Project Head Start, Volunteers in Service to America, legal Services for the Poor, and the Department of Housing and Urban Development. Medicare and Medicaid were also a Great Society legacy and are still a vital part of American life.

Topic: Lyndon Baines Johnson "What is being said about the topic?"

Main Idea: _____

2. Lake Superior is not only the largest of the five Great Lakes but is also the largest body of freshwater lakes in the world. In comparison to the other Great Lakes it is the deepest, highest above sea level, and the least polluted. The surface area is larger than South Carolina. Lake Superior contains ten percent of all the earth's fresh surface water and has as much water as all the other Great Lakes combined and even an additional two Lake Erie. Superior's shoreline, if straightened out, could connect Duluth, MN and the Bahamas Islands.

Topic: Lake Superior "What is being said about the topic?"

Main Idea: _____

3. In 1634 Anne Hutchinson, a New England Puritan religious leader, immigrated from England to Massachusetts. Her Puritan views emphasized family, devotion, education, and the Bible. After a while in the colonies, Anne altered her religious beliefs by preaching that salvation was a gift from God, and that it was a blessing and not a curse to be a woman. She also said that God communicated directly with people instead of communicating through church officials. Her differing views caused the Puritan leader, John Winthrop, to excommunicate her from the church. She moved with her family to Portsmouth, Rhode Island until her husband's death. In 1642 she moved to New York where she and all but one of her children were killed in an Indian attack.

Topic: Anne Hutchinson "What is being said about the topic?"

Main Idea: _____

4. Irving Berlin was born Israel Baline in Siberia in 1888 and came to New York with his parents. He, like thousands of other Jewish immigrants, settled in the poor area of New York's Lower East Side. He only went to school for a few years and although he never received any formal music instruction, he had many musical successes which are "icons" in American culture. Irving Berlin's "God Bless America," "Easter Parade," "White Christmas," "Blue Skies," "How Deep is the Ocean," and "Always" are but a few of the "'icons." He also wrote full length musicals, "Alexander's Ragtime Band," "Annie Get Your Gun," and "Call Me Madam." From 1910 to the early 1930s, Berlin wrote Broadway musicals and then he moved to Hollywood, CA and wrote songs for the movies. He wrote over a thousand songs during his lifetime.

Topic: Irving Berlin "What is being said about the topic"

Main Idea: _____

5. The majority of Kuwaitis have extended families. Extended families consist of a husband and his wives (according to Islam a husband can have up to four wives as long as he can afford them), his sons and their wives and children, and the unmarried sons and daughters. After the father dies, each son separates from the extended family and begins his own. Kuwaitis have a patriarchal society which means that fathers are in charge and head of the family. Marriages are mostly arranged. A preferred match is between first cousins. The extended family in Kuwait has brought support and

resiliency especially during times when Kuwait was invaded by Iraq.

Topic: Extended families in Kuwait "What is being said about the topic?"

Main Idea: _____

6. The hardest metal in the world is a diamond. In fact, oil drills have diamond tips to dig through rock. Hardness is ranked 10-1 with 10 being the hardest. Diamonds with the hardness of 10 can only be scratched by other diamonds. Because of its hardness, diamonds can be worn every day which is probably the reason it was chosen to be the symbol for engagements and weddings. Almost half of all diamonds are from Central or South Africa, while Canada, India, Russia, Brazil, and Australia produce the remaining diamonds. Lake Argyle, Africa is near the richest and largest diamond mine and this year produced a third of all the world's diamonds.

Topic: Diamonds, the hardest metal "What is being said about the topic?"

Main Idea: _____

7. An anecdote is a short account of a particular incident or event. An example of an anecdote would an amusing story. Anecdotes are a popular way to begin a speech. A few synonyms of anecdote would be "short story," "yarn," "story" or reminiscence.

Topic: Anecdote "What is being said about the topic?"

Main Idea: _____

8. Before starting a project or assignment whether it is writing a paper for English, studying for a test, or cleaning the garage, an important question should be asked: "What will my finished product look like?" This question is extremely important and it relates to an underused principle of learning…previewing. Previewing can also be thought of as anticipation, prediction, forecasting the outcome. It gives direction and helps focus attention and concentration. Next time an assignment is given, take a few moments and visualize how you imagine your finished project will look. Can't you visualize how your garage will look after cleaning it?

Topic: Previewing "What is being said about the topic?"

Main Idea: _____

Chapter Summary

The main idea connects all the information in a paragraph, section, chapter, or book. Identifying the main idea is essential for comprehending textbook material. Usually the stated main idea is in the topic sentence. The first step in understanding expository information is to identify the main idea.

Main Idea Summary
Name 3 places where main ideas might be found in paragraphs. It's OK to go back to the beginning of the chapter to find the answers.

_____   _____   _____

What are 2 questions to ask to find the main idea?

1._____

2._____

Why is it important to find the main idea?

_____

_____

Are main ideas stated, implied, or both?

_____

Give eight ways main idea questions are asked on standardized tests.

1. _____
2. _____
3. _____
4. _____
5. _____
6. _____
7. _____
8. _____

Teach It

"The best way to make sure you know something is to teach it!"

Course: All courses

Goal: To learn important information by teaching it

Material Needed: Materials you need to study for a test, paper, paper, pen

Individual or group: Group

Lesson Duration: 30-45 minutes

Finished Product to be graded: Submit your "lesson plans"

Why do I need to learn this?

A sure way to learn something is to teach it to someone else. Students like taking the part of the teacher. They prepare a lesson and then "teach it." This strategy involves selecting the material to teach, writing about it, and delivering it. It is an active strategy including reading, writing, and speaking.

Procedure

1. Assemble class notes and identify material from the textbook.

2. Create a 15-20 minute lesson and "give" your lesson to your class, a family member, or friend.

Final Thoughts

If possible, use a whiteboard and colored markers for your "lecture". Keep your lessons and use them for review. Do this strategy for all your classes.

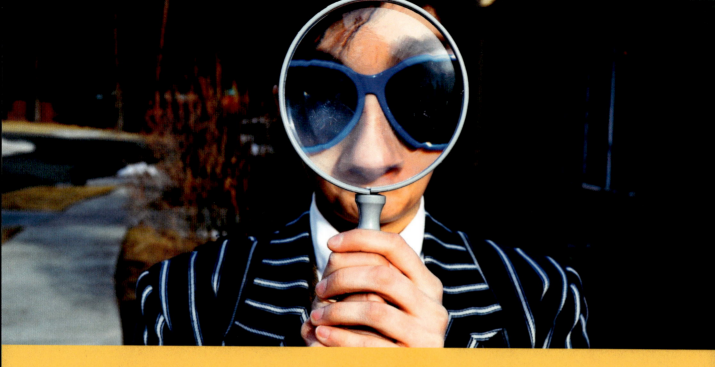

5

Attention to Details

*"The difference between something good and
something great is attention to detail."*

Charles R. Swindell

"It's the little details that are vital. Little things make big things happen."

John Wooden

"I learned no detail was too small. It was all about the details."

Brad Grey

"Success is the sum of details."

Harvey S. Firestone

"As a journalist, the details always tell the story."

James McBride

"It's attention to detail that makes the difference between average and stunning."

Francis Atterbury

"When you pay attention to detail, the big picture will take care of itself."

Georges St-Pierre

"Excellence is in the details. Give attention to details and excellence will come."

Perry Paxton

CHALLENGE 1
Learning how details support the main idea

In the second part of this chapter you will read about details

👉 Understanding how details support the main idea

👉 Identifying major and minor details

👉 Recognizing supporting details in textbooks

👉 Recognizing supporting details in standardized tests

👉 Analyzing how correct and incorrect supporting details questions are

👉 asked on standardized tests

👉 Reinforcing Supporting Details through Assignments:

👉 Writing Connection

👉 Exercises 1-5

Tupac Amaru Shakur, from Death Row Records, located on the West Coast and Christopher "Notorious B.I.G" Wallace (also known as Biggie Smalls) of the Bad Boy Records on the East Coast will forever be recognized as the two faces for what is known today as the east coast and West Coast controversy.

The sentence you just read is a topic sentence that states the main idea: *Tupac Shakur and Biggie Smalls will forever be associated with the East Coast West Coast controversy.*

After reading this main idea, don't you want to know more what happened to Tupac and Biggie Smalls? Don't you wish there were more details? It's the details that support the main idea that gives a story its backbone and character.

Writing Connection

Respond: Read the story on the next page. Then, on the lined paper below, write as many details that support the main idea as possible. At the end of your list of details, write what you read in other sources about the east coast west coast rivalry.

_____

_____

_____

_____

_____

_____

_____

_____

_____

_____

The Rapper's News Flash

Hip Hop as it is known was introduced in the 1980s. It rose from the state of New York with storytelling and rhymes. With striking beats and metaphors that will never be found in an English class, writers turned their life stories into songs. Artist such as KRSOne, Public Enemy, Slick Rick, although originally from London, and don't forget the fathers of rap, Run DMC, paved the way for the future rappers that we hear on the radio today. By the 1990s a spinoff of hip hop was introduced and this style of rap was known as Gangsta Rap. Gangsta Rap, unlike hip hop, had a rough edge; it wasn't about using metaphors or projecting an educational political message. The stories that were being told were of hardships, street life and pain. The music now was raw and uncut and coming from the West Coast, in addition to the East coast which was its original birth. The two most iconic artists, Tupac Amaru Shakur, from Death Row Records, located on the west coast and Christopher "Notorious B.I.G" Wallace (also known as Biggie Smalls) of the Bad Boy Records on the East Coast will forever be recognized as the two faces for what is known today as the East Coast and West Coast controversy.

The irony behind this East Coast and West Coast controversy is that Tupac was originally from the East Coast. The East Coast is where he developed his passion for writing and love for rhyming. It was in New York where he and Biggie Smalls formed a friendship that later turned into a feud. When Tupac was nineteen he and his family moved to Marion County, California. That was the beginning to the end. Family life for Tupac wasn't the best and he turned to the streets for comfort. His songs, now coming from the West Coast became extremely popular among the youth. Tupac sold over 75 million albums. On September 7, 1996 Tupac was shot four times in the chest and died six days later. His death raised suspicion of West Coast rappers.

Biggie Smalls began releasing remixes with rhyme and rap in early 1994. His first album was released on September of 1994 and eventually reached the top of the billboard. The album was eventually certified four times platinum. Small's success came at the time when the West Coast hip hop was prominent in the charts which shifted the focus back to the East Coast. The fight for dominance on the charts between the East Coast and West Coast rappers became hyped.

In March of 1997, The Notorious B.I.G., Biggie Smalls, left the East Coast to travel to California to promote his album. He was shot and killed by an unknown assailant. Many felt it was retaliation for the death of Tupac.

Introduction

A typical paragraph has a topic, main idea, and many supporting details. In fact, most paragraphs in your college textbooks are full of supporting details which explain, describe, and reinforce the main idea. Details add interesting facts to a topic and/or main idea and make it more understandable, comprehensible, and complete.

👉 **You need to know many details associated with topics and main ideas to help you score well on exams.**

👉 **Your professor assumes you know the main idea so most exams questions will ask for details.**

Understanding how details support the main idea

Now that you understand main ideas, it is important to know how authors support the main idea so the receiver can fully understand the message and not be left with a general statement.

👉 **The author uses supporting details to clarify the main idea and continue the thought.**

👉 **Supporting details are specifics that an author uses to expand on, develop and support the main idea. These details are examples, facts, ideas, illustrations, cases, anecdotes, reasons, and evidence.**

There are two types of details. **Major details** are the most important details and directly support the main idea whereas **minor details**, although important, are not as essential as major details. Basically, they provide interesting, additional information to the major supporting details.

The author's choice of supporting details is shaped by the nature of the topic and the purpose of the message. For example, in the news report on the previous page about the East Coast West Coast rapper conflict, the author wanted to provide facts about both sides of the dispute. Thus, the author supported the main idea with facts. In another situation, if the author were describing a beautiful vacation, the supporting details would have examples and illustrations. The courses in the field of psychology, social work and nursing usually use detailed case studies to support the main idea.

Identifying major and minor details

As discussed in the introduction, major details support the main idea and minor supporting details support a major detail. It is important to remember that identifying the supporting details of the main idea means to select a detail that directly supports the main idea. However, identifying minor details means to select a detail only if it supports a major detail. Think of it this way: Suppose you are outlining a chapter in a textbook. Your heading and topic would be your main idea and Roman numeral one. The support of the topic is your major supporting detail which you would place indented under Roman numeral one as "a". An example of this major detail would be placed indented under "a" as "1". This example is your minor detail. Determining major from minor details is similar to outlining the selection.

I Main Idea
   a. Major Detail
   b. Major detail
      1. Minor Detail
      2. Minor Detail
   c. Major Detail

II Main Idea
   a. Major Detail
      1. Minor Detail
      2. Minor Detail
   b. Major Detail

 Read the sample exercise below. Then read the analysis. Note the supporting details and minor details in the selection. Look at the outline and vision how you might outline this paragraph.

Analyze this

American kickball is an old favorite that was popular with youngsters in the 1960's and 1970's. It is now played by adults and is gaining momentum as an over 40 active sport. Kickball rules are closely related to those of baseball which is a major factor that helped in the popularity. The main difference is that in baseball a softball is used and in kickball a large rubber ball is used. The kickball is about the size of a basketball and the softball is harder and smaller. Like baseball, kickball is played on a baseball diamond with 4 bases arranged in the corners of the diamond with the home base located on one of the diamonds. They both have an infield and an outfield which players have positions of retrieving or catching the ball and tagging the opponent team out. The outfield mainly retrieves the ball when it is kicked out pass the infield. The infield catches the ball and tries to tag the runner out who is running toward base. However, the main difference in the two sports is that baseball has a batter that hits the ball with a bat and kickball has a kicker who kicks the ball when it is rolled to him by the pitcher.

Kickball

I. Kickball is becoming popular
      a. Kickball was popular with youngsters during the 60's and 70's
      b. Kickball is gaining popularity with those over 40 years of age.
      c. Kickball rules are closely related to baseball
II. Difference and similarities in Kickball and Baseball
      a. In baseball a softball is used.
            1. The softball is harder and smaller
      b. In kickball a larger ball is used
            1. The kickball is about the size of a basketball.
      c. Both kickball and baseball are played on a diamond with 4 bases
            1. The bases are placed in the corner of the diamond
      d. Both have an infield and an outfield
            1. In these positions the players catch balls and tag the opponent team out.
            2. The outfield retrieves and catches the ball when it passes infield
            3. The infield catches the ball and tags the runner out
      e. Home plate player is one of the major differences
            1. Baseball has a batter where the ball is thrown to him or her by a pitcher
            2. Kickball has a kicker where the ball is rolled to him or her by a pitcher

Analysis

You can see from the outline that the main idea is:

• Who or what is the paragraph about? Kickball

• What is happening with the who or what? It is becoming popular and has differences and similarities to baseball.

Main Idea

Kickball is becoming popular and has differences and similarities to baseball.

• The five major supporting details are supported by minor supporting details. For example line "a" states, "in baseball, a softball is used," is a major supporting detail supported by a minor detail, "the softball is harder and smaller." Let's look at another example. "In kickball, a larger ball is used," is a major supporting detail which is supported by a minor detail, "the kickball is about the size of a basketball." The key to supporting details is that major supporting details support the main idea and minor supporting details support the major details. In the outline, lines a-e are major supporting details that support the main idea. The indented lines are under the major details are minor details that only support the major detail as an example.

This paragraph is supported by major and minor details. The major details offer four facts about popularity of kickball. The other supporting major details offer examples of how kickball is different and similar to baseball. Each of these five examples are supported by minor details that expand on and develop the major supporting details.

Supporting details have seven primary functions. They are:

1. To define the topic such as it is done in a dictionary;

2. To give examples and an attempt to further explain or help the receiver understand the topic;

3. To describe the topic so that the reader can picture the topic;

4. To give reasons of supporting an argument or opinion;

5. To explain a fact or idea;

6. To present a sequence of events;

7. To help the discovery of the character through description.

"When I was a little boy, they called me a liar; but now that I am grown up, they call me a writer."
Isaac Bashevis Singer

Recognizing supporting details in textbooks

We have all had the experience of reading our text and highlighting or marking every detail in the text as equally important. The problem is that as we read, we forget to ask ourselves which details are important and which are not important! In other words, which details are significant and should be marked and which details are not significant and don't need to be marked. It is rare that a professor will test on a minutiae detail. As a student becomes more and more knowledgeable about the topic, he/she will become more discerning about which details are important and which ones are less important. Other than using a reading comprehension strategy like Outline by Heading, one way to judge significance is to use a significance/importance checklist below. Put a check next to each item you answered "yes."

Questions that help determine if the supporting detail is significant/important

- ☐ This is a detail the author uses to support the topic of this section.
- ☐ This is a detail the author uses to prove a statement made earlier in the section.
- ☐ This is a detail that adds information to the topic in the section.
- ☐ This is a detail that shows the opposing view of the topic in the section.
- ☐ This is a detail that supports other details in a significant way.
- ☐ This is a detail that helps me understand the topic.
- ☐ This is a detail that provides information for me to draw a conclusion.
- ☐ This is a detail that provides information for me to make an inference.
- ☐ This is a detail that provides information for me to define a term or concept.
- ☐ This is a detail that provides information for me to make an inference.

Recognizing supporting details in standardized tests

Since all reading material has main ideas and supporting details, it is practically a certainty that a standardized test would have supporting detail questions. On most tests, supporting detail questions will not use the word "supporting detail" or "detail" in the question stem. Instead the questions will be asked in the following way.

1. All of the following are factors that support the main idea except…?

2. Which factor supports the main idea?

3. Which factor supports the major supporting idea of_____?

4. The author uses which of the following to illustrate_____?

5. According the to the passage or paragraph _____is a reason for_____?

Analyzing how correct and incorrect supporting detail questions are asked on standarized tests

Passages on standardized tests usually come from textbooks, independent writers, lectures, essays, newspapers, magazines, or made up by the text makers. The level of difficulty is usually college level and prior knowledge of the passage subject is usually not necessary. To keep the test standardized and uniform, correct options are usually worded one way and incorrect options usually fall into 4 main categories.

Correct options:

👉 A restatement or paraphrase of a supporting detail given in the paragraph or entire passage;

👉 A restatement or paraphrase of a minor supporting detail that supports a major supporting detail.

Incorrect options:

✖ A detail, given in the passage or paragraph that does not support the topic sentence or main idea;

✖ A major detail given in the passage or paragraph that correctly supports the main idea when a minor detail that supports a major detail is sought;
i.e. The test's author lures the student in choosing a major supporting detail that supports the main idea; however, a minor supporting detail that supports the major detail is asked for and is the correct answer.

✖ A minor detail given in the passage or paragraph that correctly supports a major supporting detail when a major detail for the main idea is sought;
i.e. The test's author lures the student in choosing a minor supporting detail that supports a major detail: however, a major supporting detail
✖ that supports the main idea is asked and is the correct answer;

A closely related detail that is not contained within the passage or paragraph.

Reinforcing supporting details through assignments

Writing Connection

Read the excerpt from "Great Expectations" on page 143 before you do this writing assignment. Pip thought that Miss Havisham was "the strangest lady, I have ever seen." <u>Of all the details in this selection, choose the 5 that you think are</u> the reason Pip said this. Explain your answer by writing 1-2 paragraphs with specific details and examples.

Exercise 1: Writing specific details

Read each main idea sentence and write two sentences that have details which support the main idea sentence. Read the example and notice how supporting details "back up," provide facts, define, describe, or support the main idea.

Example:
Today's children spend too much time watching TV or playing electronic games.

Details:
1. Many children are becoming obese because of inactivity.
2. TV and video games take time away from reading and homework.

1. Student athletes earn their scholarships.
   a._____
   b._____

2. When designing a park, the designer should consider people of all ages.
   a._____
   b._____

3. The White House is especially beautiful in the spring.
   a._____
   b._____

4. The members of the rock band look strange.
   a._____
   b._____

5. I love to eat at the new fast food restaurant.
   a._____
   b._____

6. My idea of a perfect vacation is two weeks at a fancy resort on the beach.
   a._____
   b._____

7. My mom's house is very comfortable but looks quite old fashioned.
   a._____
   b._____

8. Jane is becoming more self-centered and I'm not surprised she has no friends.

a._____

b._____

9. The third grade teacher shows concern for all students.

a._____

b._____

10. The host of the Oscar Awards tried to be funny but he "bombed out".

a._____

b._____

Exercise 2: Mapping supporting details

Read each main idea sentence and write two sentences that have details which support the main idea sentence. Read the example and notice how supporting details "back up," provide facts, define, describe, or support the main idea.

<u>Example:</u>

Controlling childhood obesity begins at home and at school. Parents should set a good example by making sure the family eats dinner together, buying unprocessed, healthful food for balanced meals, limiting sedentary activities such as TV and electronic games, and encouraging more calorie burning activities. Schools need to teach nutrition in the lower grades and review healthy eating habits often. Schools also need to provide at least thirty minutes of daily exercise such as recess and physical education at least three times a week. Finally, cafeteria food and vending machine selections must provide healthful and nutritious meals and snacks.

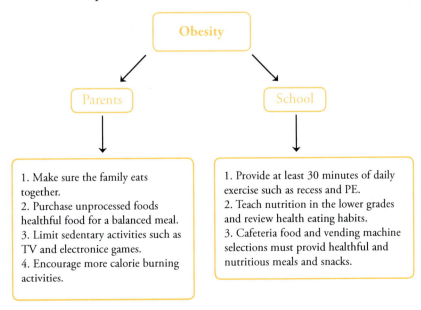

1. Ray Charles was a brilliant musician credited along with Louis Jordan and Sam Cooke for the crossover of black artists to mainstream music in the 1950s. Some say he is responsible for developing soul music by merging rhythm and blues with gospel. He was born in poverty and at age five became blind. At this early age, he began to play piano and went to St. Augustine School for the Deaf and Blind where he studied composition and learned to write music in Braille. He accomplishments are many and his fame is as widespread as Billy Holliday and Elvis Presley. Some of his well-known hits are "Ruby," "I Got a Woman," "What'd I Say?," "Georgia On My Mind," "Hit the Road, Jack," "Your Cheating Heart," and "You Are My Sunshine."

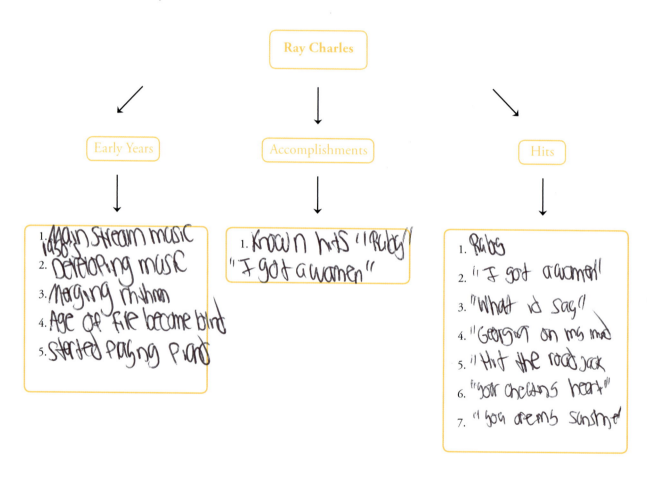

Ray Charles

Early Years

Accomplishments

Hits

1. Main Stream music 1950's
2. Developing music
3. Merging rhythm
4. Age of five became blind
5. Started playing piano

1. Known hits "Ruby" "I got a women"

1. Rubs
2. "I got a woman"
3. "What id say"
4. "Georgia on my mind"
5. "Hit the road jack"
6. "your cheatns heart"
7. "you arems sunsine"

2. Central Park is an 843 acre park located in Manhattan in the center of New York City. It borders are 59th to 110th Streets and Fifth to Eighth Avenue. In the late 1859s New York officials wanted a public park to rival the parks in Paris and London. The land designated for the park was a swampy area where newcomers and European immigrants came and built temporary shanties. The architects, Fredrick Law Olmstead and Calvert Vaux, created "The Greenswards Plan" which took 15 years to complete. The goal was to create a public park where both the lower and upper classes could enjoy a beautiful place to relax or participate in activities. Several hundred thousand trees were planted to "block out" the tall buildings bordering the park. Today the park has a lake, pond, zoo, skating rink, English style gardens, hills, winding paths, bridges, playgrounds, and sports fields. Every day there are events planned such as biking excursions, lectures, bird watching, exhibits, art shows, concerts, and sporting events. Central Park was the first landscaped park in the United States. In 1963 it became a National Historical landmark. The park is open all year, it is the most visited park in the US with 25 million visitors annually.

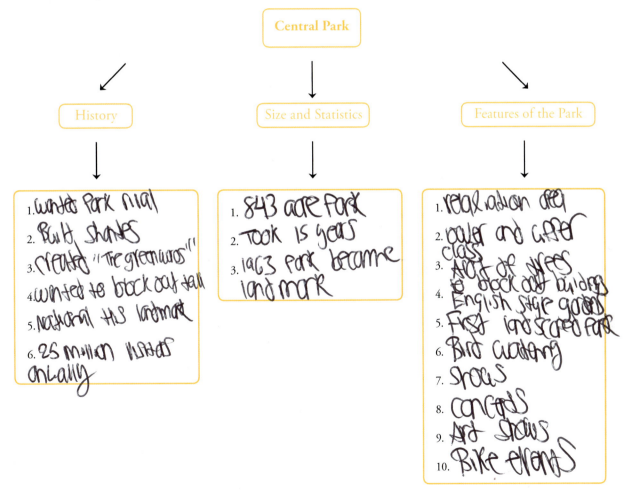

3. Many, if not most, college students are going to have stress when final exams are approaching. Start to prepare about three weeks before the exam week to get a good head start. About three weeks before the final exam, assemble all notes, textbook readings, handouts, and old tests. Form a study group and divide the material among the members. Each member has the responsibility to teach the group his/her assigned material. Set up dates and times and write this in your organizer. Be sure to reread your syllabus because you might get some hints about the final. Two weeks before the final, keep fitting new information into your study material. Review daily until most material becomes at the "automatic level." One week before the final, predict test questions. Use index cards for material you intend to memorize and use the cards to keep testing yourself. Don't forget to reflect or think about the material in-between study sessions. Keep asking yourself, "If I were the professor, what would I expect my students to know for the final?"

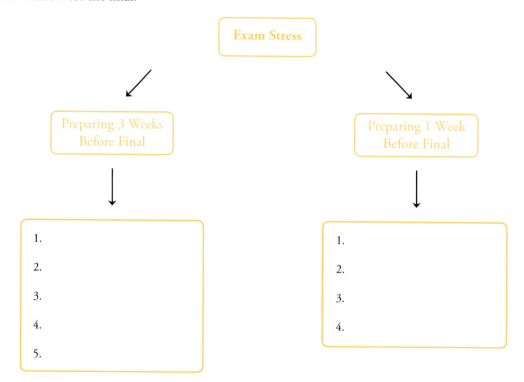

4. Japan has a robust economy in spite of the fact the country has very few natural resources. How were the Japanese able to accomplish this high level economy since the 1950s? Japan must import raw material and convert these to finished, high quality manufactured products to meet the demands of their consumers. Some products sold worldwide are automobiles, electronics, computers, petrochemicals, pharmaceuticals, ships, aerospace products, textiles, and processed food. Japan exports 97% of its manufactured goods. The materials that are imported to produce these goods are mainly fuel, ores and metals, and other raw materials. There are cultural factors of the Japanese that also contribute to Japan's manufacturing economy. Among them are the homogeneity of its population, a high level of education, skilled labor, advanced technology, and a government which provides financial incentives.

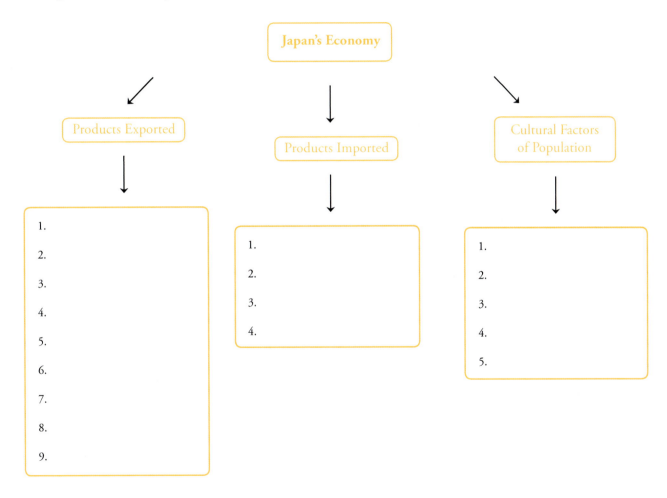

Japan's Economy

Products Exported

1.
2.
3.
4.
5.
6.
7.
8.
9.

Products Imported

1.
2.
3.
4.

Cultural Factors of Population

1.
2.
3.
4.
5.

5. White collar criminals are usually highly respected people with status in the community who use their authority and position to commit crimes for personal gain. These crimes are different from the typical street crimes because most of the criminals are educated, come from a privileged background, are intelligent, and usually there is no threat of physical force or violence. Some of the white collar crimes are insider trading, bribery, forgery, fraud, embezzlement, computer crimes, and identity crimes. Examples of white collar criminals are Bernard Madoff, Allen Stanford and executives from Enron. White collar crimes cost the U.S. more than three billion dollars annually.

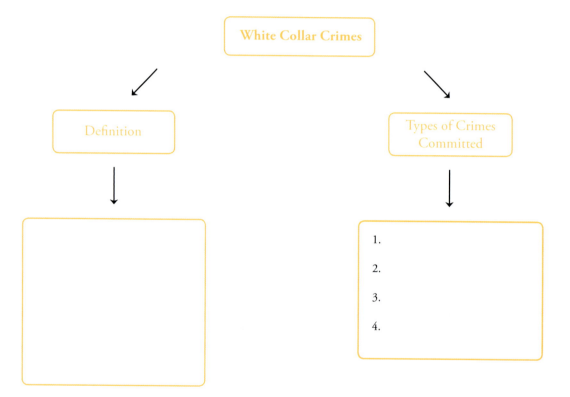

6. Fifty years ago there were two types of dogs, pedigrees and mixed breeds (also called mutts). Today there is a third type of dog called a Designer Dog which is in demand. Although Designer Dogs are crossbreeds, also known as hybrids (they are bred purebred to purebred), they are not a breed recognized by the American Kennel Club. This crossbreed or hybrid dog differs from a mixed breed because the ancestry is known and owners will have a good idea of how the dog will look as an adult dog. They have become popular for many reasons. Some people think Designer Dogs are easier to train than any other breeds, many are hypoallergenic, healthier, make great companions, are trendy, and for the most part, are very unique and cute. Some of the most common Designer Dogs are the Labradoodles, the Goldendoodles, Cocapoos, Peekapoos, Schnoodles, Yorkipoos, Sheltipoos, Maltipoos, and Shihpoos. As you can see the "poo" Designer Dogs are bred from the Poodle which are desired for their intelligence and hypoallergenic coat, combined with the personality of the other breed. If you are considering a Designer Dog in the future, there is one more thing to know, they often cost more than purebreds.

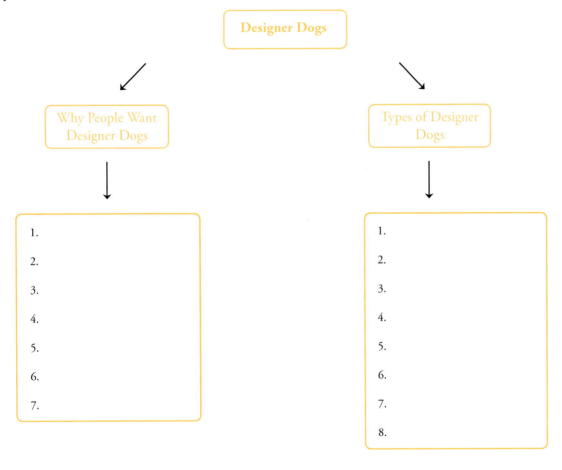

7. Lisa Scott, author of *It's All About Him: How to Identify and Avoid the Narcissistic Male Before You Get Hurt*, claims that narcissism is an epidemic in our society. Identifying narcissistic behavior before a relationship gets serious is extremely important. The American Psychological Association has nine traits, five of which need to be present to determine if someone has a Narcissistic Personality Disorder. The first trait is that the person feels grandiose and self-important for reasons not supported by reality; the second is an obsession with fantasies about unlimited success, fame, power, or omnipotence; the third is the belief he or she is unique and special and can only relate to other people who are also unique and special. The fourth is that the person needs excessive adulation, attention, and affirmation; fifth, this person also has a sense of entitlement; sixth, a narcissist will exploit others without guilt or remorse, seventh, is devoid of empathy, eighth, displays arrogant and haughty behavior, and lastly, is jealous of others, yet has a fragile self-esteem: Scott concludes by saying that if you suspect your mate is a narcissist, it is time to either learn to live with him/her or else move on!

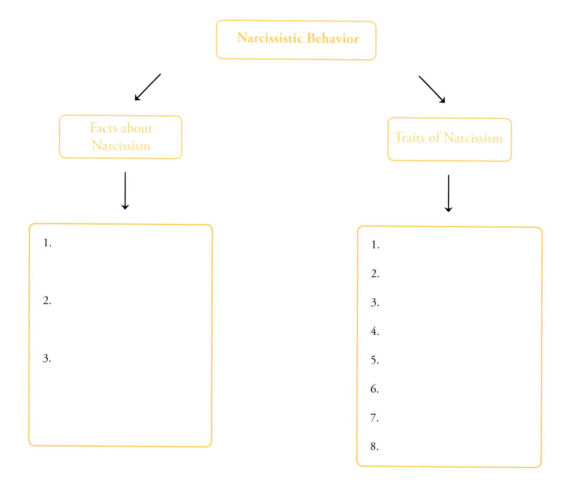

Narcissistic Behavior

Facts about Narcissism

Traits of Narcissism

1.

2.

3.

1.

2.

3.

4.

5.

6.

7.

8.

8. Edgar Allen Poe was orphaned at age two when his mother died. He lived with a foster family who provided him with the best education possible but not with the family life or security that he desperately wanted. As a result, Edgar was often miserable, lonely and depressed. He did, however, find solace in literature, especially in the work of Percy Shelly, William Wordsworth, Moliere, and Lord Byron. Edgar attended University of Virginia where he started to write poetry. His foster father did not support Edgar's writing and insisted he get a business degree. Edgar left college to pursue writing when his foster father stopped contributing toward college. The rest of Poe's life was tumultuous and some of the misery he experienced is reflected in his writings. He was best known for short stories and poetry which were full of mystery, the macabre, and science fiction. He was paid only nine dollars for "The Raven" which appeared with great success in the Evening Mirror. Besides "The Raven," his most famous works are "The Black Cat," "The Tell-Tale Heart," "The Purloined Tale," "Annabel Lee," "Eulalie," and "The City in the Sea." Poe died at age forty-one.

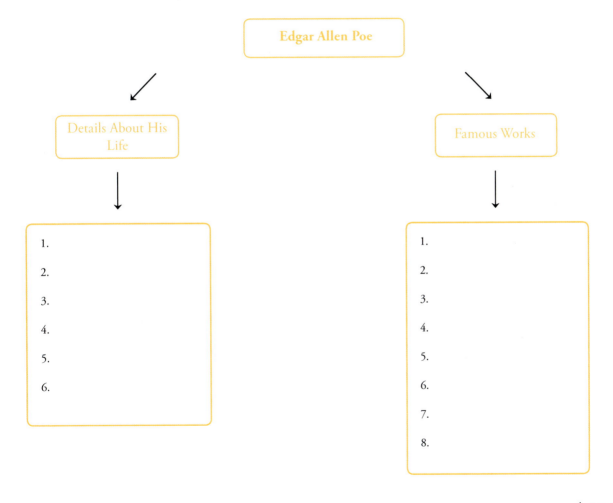

Edgar Allen Poe

Details About His Life

1.

2.

3.

4.

5.

6.

Famous Works

1.

2.

3.

4.

5.

6.

7.

8.

Exercise 3: Outlining Specific Details

Outlining is similar to mapping but instead of using maps, you will write the missing major or minor details under the topic. Read each passage and complete the outline with details. Answers may vary depending on the number of details you want to include.

1. Jane Austen, one of the most beloved English authors of all times, was born in 1775 and died in 1817. Today, fans of her novels and films identify with her characters and stories about finding suitable marriage partners. The novels are centered around intelligent women living in England at a time when family rank determined one's social status. During her 42 years she wrote six major novels. *Pride and Prejudice, Sense and Sensibility,* and *Emma* are three of the most popular. Jane was the daughter of a clergyman and part of a close knit family. She never married and lived with her family all her life. She was especially close to her sister and confidant, Cassandra. Both girls attended school until her father could no longer afford to send them so he educated the children and encouraged Jane's writing. It is ironic that although Jane never married, she understood and wrote about deep feelings and romantic relationships. Her novels always had happy endings!

Main Idea: Jane Austen is a beloved English author.

Major Detail:

1. Jane's family life

      a. _____

      b. _____

2. _____

      a. *Pride and Prejudice*

      b. *Emma*

      c. _____

3. Characteristics of Austen's novels

      a. intelligent women

      b. _____

      c. _____

2. Did you realize that the seven huge landmasses or the seven continents are always slowly moving? This movement is called the Continental Drift. About 220 million years ago the seven continents were one huge continent known as Pangaea which is a Greek word meaning "all lands." Twenty million years later the one land mass divided into two continents and 65 million years later the continents again separated into the seven continents of today. However, the seven continents are still moving very slowly and in 150 million years from now our seven continents may look very different. Historians point out how Arabia split apart from Africa. The Red Sea was the dividing line that split the land mass. Every few years the Red Sea becomes wider. The Theory of Plate Tectonics explains the shifting or Continental Drift Theory. This theory states that the plates on the ocean floor move during disruptions such as earthquakes which cause the continents to shift position.

Main Idea: The seven continents are moving because of the Continental Drift.

Major Detail:

1. 220 million years ago world was one land mass.

        a. _____
        b. _____

2. Example of how Arabia separated.

        a. _____
        b. Red Sea becomes wider every few years.
        c. _____

3. Theory of plate tectonics.

        a. _____
        b. _____

3. Many college students avoid studying with a group because they think it wastes time. However, if they join the "right study group," they will surely change their minds because the group "shares the load," and it can be enjoyable because of the interaction with classmates. The first guideline in forming a group is to find a committed, serious group of approximately five students. A second guideline is to find a group leader who will set up a schedule and who will assign each member a section of the material he or she will present to the other members. Remember, that teaching

something to someone else will heighten your understanding. Other guidelines are that meetings should start on time, important notes should be copied for members, and mock test questions should be made for each member.

Main Idea: Being part of college study group has many benefits.

Major Detail:

1. Advantages of studying with a group

      a. _____

      b. _____

2. Some guidelines when studying with a group.

      a. _____

      b. _____

      c. _____

4. Having an attractive face, a well-toned body, a sparkling personality, a high IQ, a degree from a prestigious university, a solid resume, and wearing a well-tailored suit appear to be all the essentials one would want to have for a dinner interview with a respected Fortune 500 company. These traits, however, would surely be cancelled if you left your table manners at home. A few "no-no's" are: keeping your elbows off the table, slurping your soup, talking or chewing with your mouth full, blowing your nose at the table, using the wrong piece of silverware, touching several pieces of bread before deciding on one, buttering the entire roll or piece of bread at once, and lowering your head to meet the food instead of raising the fork or spoon to your mouth. It is no wonder that many universities provide an etiquette expert to teach basic table manners to graduating students who are invited to dinner with their respective employers.

Main Idea: Table manners are very important to the graduating student.

Major Detail:

1. The bad habits you want to avoid

      a. _____

      b. _____

c. _____
d. _____
e. _____
f. _____
g. _____
h. _____

5. Louisa Rosenblatt, a reading theorist and researcher, developed the "Transactional Theory of Reading" which states that reading is a two-way interaction between the reader and the author, in other words, there is a transaction between the reader and the text. The primary purpose for reading in school is called "efferent" reading in which the reader reads textbooks to "get the facts" or "to carry away the facts." Rosenblatt says another kind of reading is "aesthetic" in which the reader uses his/her senses, imaginations, and feelings that will "fuse the cognitive and affective elements of the consciousness - sensations, images, feelings, ideas - into a personally lived through poem or story." Both kinds of reading need to be learned and practiced for competent reading.

Main Idea: Louisa Rosenblatt developed the "transactional theory of reading".

Major Detail:

1. Definition of "transactional theory of reading"

    a. _____
    b. _____

2. Efferent reading.

    a. _____
    b. _____

3. Aesthetic reading.

    a. _____
    b. _____

6. Annually, over four million people visit the most famous cemetery in the U.S., Arlington National Cemetery. Before the Civil War, General Robert E. Lee, head of the Confederate troops and his family owned the Arlington estate and land in Arlington, Virginia. On March 3, 1884,

Congress purchased Arlington from Lee for $150,000. During the Civil War northern troops occupied the land and some of the land was used as a cemetery. Shortly thereafter, on June 15, 1984, Secretary of War, Edwin M. Staunton declared part of the estate, 200 acres, would be designated as a military cemetery. Both the Northern and Southern armies are represented at Arlington. Soldiers from the Spanish American War, unidentified soldiers from all wars, soldiers reinterred from the Revolutionary War, soldiers from World Wars I and II, and the Korean War are also buried there. Famous historical people such as John F. Kennedy and his brother, Senator Robert Kennedy, are buried there. There is also a Tomb of the Unknown Soldier which has the remains of three US soldiers. This monument pays homage to all missing and unidentified US armed force military men and women. There are over twenty-seven funerals a day at Arlington.

Main Idea: Arlington National Cemetery is the cemetery for the armed forces.

Major Detail:

1. Beginnings of Arlington

       a. _____

       b. _____

2. Soldiers from many wars are buried at Arlington

       a. _____

       b. _____

       c. _____

3. Visitors to Arlington National Cemetery

       a. _____

       b. _____

       c. _____

7. Since 1914 when the Apollo Theater was built in the heart of Harlem, it has been known as "the place where stars are born and legends made." This is because on every Wednesday night since 1924, there is Amateur Night at the Apollo. One of the first amateur winners was fourteen year old Ella Fitzgerald. Bessie Smith and Billie Holliday both got their starts there in 1935. More recent artists who either appeared or got their start at

the Apollo are Stevie Wonder, Michael Jackson, James Brown, and Lauryn Hill. The next time you are in New York, City on a Wednesday, get tickets to the Apollo for amateur night.

Main Idea: The Apollo Theater has an interesting history.

Major Detail:

1. Features of the Apollo Theater

    a. _____

    b. _____

2. Famous Performers

    a. _____

    b. _____

    c. _____

    d. _____

8. Secretariat had all the qualities for a racehorse. His physique was flawless, he had impeccable bloodlines, and sportswriters often wrote he was "the quintessential running machine." Secretariat's sire was Bold Ruler and the mare was Something Royal. When he was foaled he had hips so wide the veterinarian worried he may have trouble passing the birth canal. Immediately after his birth, the vet said, "This is a whopper." During his 16 month racing career, Secretariat rose higher and faster than any horse of modern times. In 1973 Secretariat won the Triple Crown which was winning the Kentucky Derby, Preakness, and Belmont. He set the record at Belmont by winning in two minutes and twenty-four seconds, a record which still stands today. He was unanimously voted Horse of the Year, an honor which had never before given to a two-year-old horse. Secretariat died at age sixteen. The autopsy helped explain Secretariat's speed. When the veterinarian removed his heart, it was about twice the size of a normal horse's heart and a third larger than any other horse's heart he had ever seen.

Main Idea: Secretariat was a superior racehorse.

Major Detail:
1. Secretariat's qualities that made him the greatest racehorse

    a. _____

    b. _____

2. Secretariat's Accomplishments

      a. _____

      b. _____

      c. _____

3. Secretariat's death

      a. _____

      b. _____

Exercise 4: Practice/Homework

Read each main idea sentence and write two sentences that have details which support the main idea sentence.

1. A pet doesn't necessarily have to be warm and fuzzy.

a._____

b._____

2. Exercise keeps my weight under control.

a._____

b._____

3. Textbooks are much too expensive.

a._____

b._____

4. Jeans are a fashion for every age.

a._____

b._____

5. Many college students go to football games to party.

a._____

b._____

Read each passage and then complete the map with as many details as you can.

6. Many children, especially teenagers, suffer when they feel they are not as popular as they would like to be. Parents need to understand that their child's friends are among his or her most valuable possessions. Being popular is extremely important and at the high school level is probably

the most important thing in the world. School psychologists note that within a high school population there are four categories or subgroups of popularity. The popular kids are well liked by some groups and not liked by others, the amiable kids are not known well in the school but socially accepted, the neglected kids are unnoticed by everyone and some have chosen to be neglected, and finally the rejected kids are actively excluded and often bullied, and a target for verbal abuse. Many suffer the consequences of peer rejection with anger or depression. Imagine how one would feel when day after day they feel rejected and when they reach home, they vent their pent up feelings on their family.

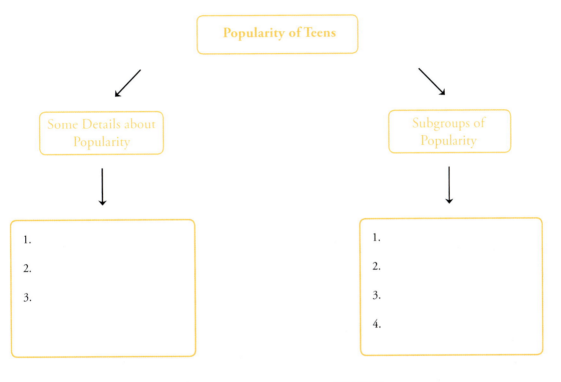

Popularity of Teens

Some Details about Popularity

1.

2.

3.

Subgroups of Popularity

1.

2.

3.

4.

Exercise 5: A selection from "Great Expectations" by Charles Dickens

The following selection is from Charles Dickens "Great Expectations." Many people say that this is their favorite part of the story. Pip is a twelve year old boy living in England during the 1850s. Although is from a poor family, he has been invited to Miss Havisham's mansion, an eccentric lady who seeks companionship with young people. Miss Havisham is a recluse (someone who lives a solitary life) who never leaves her house.

As you read this, try to visualize Pip's experience as he sees Miss Havisham in her mansion for the first time. After reading, you will be asked ten questions.

We went into the house by a side door - the great front entrance had two chains across it outside and the first thing I noticed was, that the passages were all dark, and that she had left a candle burning there. She took it up, and we went through more passages, and up a staircase, and still it was all dark, and only the candle lighted us.

At last we came to the door of a room, and she said, "Go in."

To this, she returned: "Don't be ridiculous, boy: I am not going in." And scornfully walked away, and - what was worse, took the candle with her.

This was very uncomfortable, and I was half afraid. However, the only thing to be done being to knock at the door, I knocked, and was told from within to enter. I entered, therefore, and found myself in a pretty large room, well lighted with wax candles. No glimpse of daylight was to be seen in it. It was a dressing room, as I supposed from the furniture, though much of it was of forms and uses then quite unknown to me. But prominent in it was a draped table with a gilded looking-glass, and that I made out at first sight to be a fine lady's dressing table.

Whether I should have made out this object so soon, if there had been no fine lady sitting at it, I cannot say. In an armchair, with an elbow resting on the table and her head leaning on that hand, sat the strangest lady I have ever seen, or shall ever see.

She was dressed in rich materials - satins, and lace, and silks - all of white. Her shoes were white. And she had a long white veil dependent from her

hair, and she had bridal flowers in her hair, but her hair was white. Some bright jewels sparkled on her neck and on her hands, and some other jewels lay sparkling on the table. Dresses, less splendid that the dress she wore, and half-packed trunks, were scattered about. She had not quite finished dressing, for she had but one shoe on—the other was on the table near her hand—her veil was but half arranged, her watch and chain were not put on, and some lace for her bosom lay with those trinkets, and with her handkerchief, and gloves, and some flowers, and a prayer-book, all confusedly heaped about the looking-glass.

It was not in the first moments that I saw all these things, though I saw more of them in the first moments than might be supposed. But, I saw that everything within my view which ought to be white, had been white long ago, and had lost its luster, and was faded and yellow. I saw that the bride within the bridal dress had withered like the dress, and like the flowers, and had no brightness left but the brightness of her sunken eyes. I saw that the dress had been put upon the rounded figure of a young woman, and that the figure upon whit it now hung loose, had shrunk to skin and bone. Once I had been taken to see some ghastly waxwork at the Fair, representing I know not what impossible personage lying in state. Once, I had ashes of a rich dress, that had been dug out of a vault under the church pavement. Now, waxwork and skeleton seemed to have dark eyes that moved and looked at me. I should have cried out, if I could.

"Who is it?" said the lady at the table.

"Pip, Ma'am."

"Pip?"

"Mr. Pumblechook's boy, ma'am. Come-to-play."

"Come nearer; let me look at you. Come close."

It was when I stood before her, avoiding her eyes, that I took note of the surrounding objects in details, and saw that her watch had stopped at twenty minutes to nine, and that a clock in the room had stopped at twenty minutes to nine.

"Look at me," said Miss Havisham. "You are not afraid of a woman who has never seen the sun since you were born?"

I regret to state that I was not afraid of telling the enormous lie comprehended in the answer, "No."

"Do you know what I touch here?" she said, laying her hands, one upon the other, on her left side.

"Yes, ma'm."

"What do I touch?"

"Your heart."

She uttered the word with an eager look, and with strong emphasis, and with a weird smile that had a kind of boast in it. Afterwards, she kept her hands there for a little while, and slowly took them away as if they were heavy.

"I am tired," said Miss Havisham. "I want diversion, and I am done with men and women. Play."

1. Describe Miss Havisham's dress:_____

2. Describe Miss Havisham's eyes:_____

3. What was the time on her watch?_____

4. What did Miss Havisham touch with her right hand?_____

5. In what room did Pip and Miss Havisham meet?_____

6. What had Pip seen at the Fair?_____

7. What had Miss Havisham not seen for many years?_____

8. What was in Miss Havisham's hair?_____

9. Describe Miss Havisham's jewels:_____

10. What is a looking-glass?_____

Chapter Summary

Supporting Details Summary

All communication is developed through the use of supporting details that specify, enhance, and clarify the main idea. Without details there would only be general statements that offer little insight into the topic. Supporting details continue the discussion of the main idea through examples, facts, ideas, illustrations, cases, anecdotes, reasons, and evidence. Major supporting details directly support the author's main idea and minor supporting details provide additional, information that is considered less important for comprehension. Minor supporting details support major details.

STW: Stop, Think, and then Write

"You learn to write better by reading. You learn to read better by writing. Reading and writing work together to improve your ability to think."

Unknown

Course: All courses

Goal: To maximize comprehension of reading assignments

Material Needed: Textbook and/or class notes for upcoming test, paper or small notebook, pen or pencil

Individual or group: Group

Lesson Duration: 45-60 minutes

Finished Product to be graded: Papers and notebooks that have written information from textbook

Procedure

1. Gather all material you need to study for upcoming test.

2. Take 2-5 minutes and read a section or a few paragraphs and stop reading.

3. Close your eyes and think about what you just read. If you are unable to remember most of the information, read the section again, close your eyes and think again about what you just read.

4. Cover the section you just read and write as much as you remember.

5. Repeat steps 1-4 Try to do this strategy for one hour. Use your written summaries for review.

Final Thoughts

When we take the time to "think" after learning something, we can easily assimilate the new information with our existing information. Thinking deeply about a subject helps us reach a high level of comprehension.

6

Advancing to College Writing

"Between the pages of a book is a wonderful place to be."

Anonymous

A scene from the University Student Center

Al: "How ya doing, buddy? You look down in the dumps."

Stan: "Oh! I'm feeling pretty rotten. I have a five page paper due in my psychology class tomorrow and I'm worried because I don't have enough information."

Al: "How much information do you actually have?"

Stan: "Enough for about three and a half pages."

Al: "No problem. Do what I do. It works every time. Make a great looking cover page with beautiful fonts and colorful borders. This will be a great first impression. Then use big fonts, extra spacing, and wide margins. If your teacher says anything negative about this, tell him or her you want to make it easy to read."

Stan: "Al, what a great idea! You are such a friend."

Al: "Relax, I'm not through. I just thought of something else - did you save any of your old papers? I'm into recycling. Find an old paper you did a few years ago and recycle! Here's my last bit of advice - don't try to be too clever and creative because most teachers don't have 'our kind' of humor!"

2 weeks later

Stan: "Al, I did what you said and I got my paper back and my grade was a D. The comment was, 'Not enough information.' You're right, most teachers don't have 'our kind' of humor!"

In high school you were taught how to write the basic five-paragraph essay. You learned how to arrange your ideas and facts into a nicely formulated structure. Writing in college continues with the basics you learned in high school but goes beyond the five paragraph structure. For example, in college you can have as many paragraphs as needed. Furthermore, high school essays typically have three main points whereas college essays will usually have more, and college assignments involve more critical thinking and analysis.

In this chapter you will learn:

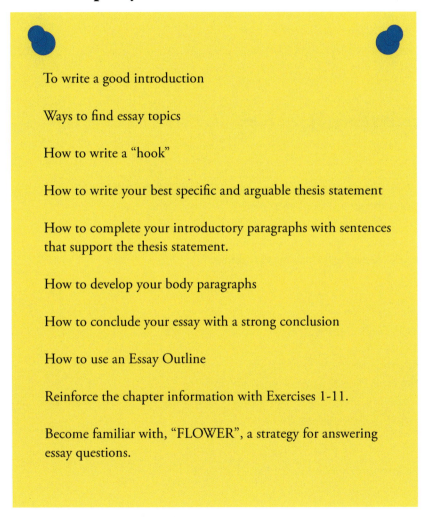

To write a good introduction

Ways to find essay topics

How to write a "hook"

How to write your best specific and arguable thesis statement

How to complete your introductory paragraphs with sentences that support the thesis statement.

How to develop your body paragraphs

How to conclude your essay with a strong conclusion

How to use an Essay Outline

Reinforce the chapter information with Exercises 1-11.

Become familiar with, "FLOWER", a strategy for answering essay questions.

Introduction

Students often struggle when assigned to write an essay. The word "essay" is from the French verb, essayer, and it means "to try." In an essay, you are trying to get your reader to see your point of view; you will need to bring your ideas to life in the reader's mind. Fortunately, you have numerous ways to achieve this goal, starting with a strong introduction which will get your reader's attention.

When you've been given your first essay assignment, it's time to improve your writing ability. Developing your writing skills, like developing skills in other areas, becomes better with the amount and quality of practice. When you are a college senior it will be satisfying to look over your freshman essays and notice the progress you have made as a writer.

CHALLENGE 1
Writing a strong introductory essay paragraph

The introduction is as important to your essay as the first few minutes in a job interview. Your first goal is to catch the attention of your reader. A strong introductory paragraph can make or break your essay. It is your only chance to make a great first impression. Readers are busy, here is the place to show them why they should take some time and pay attention to your essay.

Find a boring introductory paragraph and discuss how to make it better.

After you have decided on a topic, you can begin planning the introductory paragraph, the body of the essay, and the conclusion.

The introductory paragraph has three parts: the hook, two or more sentences that provide detail about the topic, and the thesis statement.

The body of the essay has several paragraphs that support the thesis statement.

The conclusion is the last paragraph which ends the essay with concluding remarks that support the thesis.

Finding an essay topic

Your instructor may assign a topic or you may have to find one on your own. Although an essay prompt gives you freedom to select a topic, it can be overwhelming. Hopefully, you will arrive at a topic which truly interests you and that you will enjoy learning more about, as well as exploring through writing. Choosing topics can begin by discussing ideas with your friends and family.

These questions can help select the right topic

 Do you often discuss current events?

 Are you interested in history?

 What are you thinking about majoring in college?

 What are some current social trends?

Remember to talk to your professor with questions you may have about a topic. You will also have to consider the number of pages your essay needs to be.

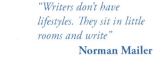

"Writers don't have lifestyles. They sit in little rooms and write"
Norman Mailer

Exercise 1: Topic Selection

Brainstorm 5 topics per category:

Current Events:
1._____
2._____
3._____
4._____
5._____

Historical Events:
1._____
2._____
3._____
4._____
5._____

College Majors I'm considering
1._____
2._____
3._____
4._____
5._____

Exercise 2: Selecting a Topic

From your lists in Exercise 1, fill in items 1-3

1. One topic I "brainstormed" from current events I want to know more about is

_____

Three questions I would ask about this topic are:

a._____
b._____
c._____

2. One topic I "brainstormed" from historical events I want to know more about is_____

Three questions I would ask about this topic are:

a._____
b._____
c._____

3. One topic I "brainstormed" from college majors I want to know more about is_____

Three questions I would ask about this topic are:

a._____
b._____
c._____

Exercise 3: Matching Topics and Subjects

Additional topic choices can come from using subject listings on your public or college library pages. Headings will range from all disciplines such as Education, Public Health, Political Science, Sociology, Medicine, and Fine Arts to name a few.

Match the following library database headings with the article you would possibly find in a search of that heading. Enter the article letter next to the category.

1. Art and Art History____
2. Business ____
3. Geography____

a. Sibling Behaviors and Birth Order
b. Plasticity of the Brain
c. Google: How Creative Companies Innovate

4. History_____
5. Kinesiology____
6. Music____
7. Neuroscience____
8. Public Health____
9. Political Science____
10. Sociology____

d. Understanding the Mechanics of Running
e. The Rise of Diabetes in the U.S.
f. Chinese Sculptured Artifacts
g. The Study of Icelandic Trends
h. Lessons from the Space Program
i. Remaking Miami - How a Place Evolves
j. A Study of Pandora vs Spotify

(Answers: 1. G, 2. C, 3. J, 4. I,5. E, 6. D,7. B,8. F,9. H, 10. A)

Begin Thinking About a "Hook"

The first sentence in your introduction contains the "hook" and is probably the most important sentence in the essay. The "hook" is a "dramatic opener" whose purpose is to "grab the reader" so he or she will continue reading. Although there is no "rule" as to when you should create the "hook", most writers begin thinking about it after they have selected the topic, however, it can be created any time during the writing process.

Options for a "hook"	Example
A quotation	The Dalai Lama said, "My religion is very simple. My religion is kindness."
A question	"Why is there an overrepresentation of inmates in our prison who cannot read?"
A definition	"Kenneth" is the name for a guy who is a chic magnet. He is the nicest guy you'll ever meet. He's smart, slightly nerdy, but funny and cute at the same time.
An anecdote	To the outside world we were a perfect family. But, the perfection seen by our friends, family, and neighbors was a hoax, a lie, and a tragedy.

Options for a "hook"	Example
Something humorous	When NASA first began sending astronauts into space, they faced a small problem. Their ballpoint pens would not work in space. They spent a decade and twelve million dollars designing a pen that would work below three hundred degrees and in space. Roscosmos (Russian Aviation and Space Agency) used a pencil.

Song lyrics	"Don't Blame Me" is a classic, popular song written over eighty years ago. Many young people keep those lyrics popular today and say those same words at least three times a day.
A familiar saying	"It's easier to catch a fly with sugar than with vinegar."
An analogy	"Human is to oxygen as plant is to carbon dioxide."
A fact	"Miami Beach has the most number of Art Deco buildings than any other city in the U.S.
A statistic	In a major educational study of 65 countries for Economic Co-operation reported that South Korea had the highest scores in reading and math. Only two countries scored higher in science—Finland and Japan.

Exercise 4: Write a "hook" for these topics. Use a different option for each "hook."

How to encourage attendance at college basketball games

Our school should offer more online courses.

There should be mandatory child rearing classes for new parents.

College athletes should receive stipends.

The U.S., like Israel, should have mandatory six months of military service for all 18 year olds citizens.

Creating your best thesis

What is a thesis statement?
A thesis is a **specific and arguable statement** that makes a claim and gives evidence to support the claim. A thesis statement is persuasive and tries to prove a point with examples and thoughtful analysis.

You may need help in creating your thesis in an essay assignment. You may need to ask your instructor exactly what it is that should be explored and supported.

As a college writer, before your essay is completed, your thesis is considered a working thesis. As you write and research, you may change the thesis based on the new information or new perspective.

What are the characteristics of a thesis statement? A thesis statement...

- is one complete sentence and is never the first sentence.

- is a convincing, argumentative statement that identifies and summarizes your point of view.

- conveys something important and guides your paper.

- avoids stating the obvious and challenges the reader to think and become engaged with the topic.

Examples of arguable thesis statements
Repeated and undocumented concussions should be reason enough for parents to prohibit their children from playing football.

View taking a reading/ writing course as an opportunity!

Think about it: how do thesis statements compare to topic sentences?

The fast food industry, along with unmindful parents, are largely responsible for the rampant child obesity epidemic in our society.

Playing video games takes too much time away from homework for most high school and college students.

The international college internship programs, although expensive, are worth the money especially for international business majors.

Although helpful and necessary for navigating professional life and connecting with friends and family, overuse of technology contributes to health problems of college freshmen.

Grocery stores in affluent neighborhoods are much better and less expensive than grocery stores in poor neighborhoods.

High school and college instructors are largely to blame for the widespread academic dishonesty found in all academic institutions.

Baseball players are the more highly skilled athletes than are football or basketball athletes.

Pre-law students should take two undergraduate courses in critical thinking, reasoning and logic to prepare them for the rigors of law school.

The United States should abolish daylight savings time because we are no longer have an agrarian society.

Country life is better than city life.

Internet service should be free for everyone.

 ## Read the examples and then think about them

Further examples: Take note of the comments after each thesis statement

1. Modern relationships evolve with popular culture and technological advancements and, therefore, these relationships are now more heavily dependent on social media and dating apps. (This thesis argues that there is a connection between relationships and changes in technology.)

2. The use of the internet as an escape from dealing with social.

interactions face-to-face has turned dating into a superficial process that sours the reputation of our technology-reliant generation. (This thesis is specific and takes an arguable stance. It shows how a large picture phenomenon has affected a generation who, although reliant on technology, may not participate in the "escape…superficial process" and have their reputation affected.)

3. Technology has cause a shift in society's thought of relationships as permanent to the thought of them as temporary. (This thesis is going in the direction of summary; the argument part is that "technology has caused…" It can be more specific and give more points of exploration for the essay.)

4. Social media can begin to become addictive and potentially lead to isolation because it can consume one's life and begin to run your life. (This thesis is interesting and could be better if it were more specific.)

5. Some people become so involved with their online persona, that they end up forgetting who they really are. They use this persona to create someone who isn't dealing with the problems they have to deal with. (Watch out for casual language and repetition: "deal with"/"dealing". When a thesis grows to two sentences, you can reword and use a semicolon to help the reader understand which part is your essay argument.)

"Get it down. Take chances. It may be bad but it's the only way you can do anything really good."
William Faulkner

Exercise 5: Is the thesis specific and arguable? Yes or No. Check your answers with the discussion that follows.

1. In the short story, "The Story of the Hour," the most important literary elements are description and surprise._____

2. The short story,
"The Story of an Hour." Is about a seemingly normal day in the character's life._____

3. Junot Diaz is an important American fiction writer._____

4. Readers should pay close attention to Junot Diaz's uses of dialogue, irony, and language._____

5. Gabriel Garcia Marquez asks his readers to enter a world where the impossible happens. _____

6. Magical realism is a confusing literary genre. _____

7. One can find a connection between American's health and nutritional choices. _____

8. Ohio high school students are being let down by school menu decision makers; their health and academic success remain at stake._____

9. College students should take advantage of publication opportunities with *The New York Times* because of the practical experience, networking opportunities, and resume additions._____

10. *The New York Times* offers writing opportunities to college students. _____

 # Discussion

1. In the short story, "The Story of the Hour," the most important literary elements are description and surprise. (This works as a thesis because you can now discuss/argue your point of view of how description and surprise are most important in this story by providing examples to illustrate your claims.)

2. The short story, "The Story of an Hour," is about a seemingly normal day in the character's life. (This thesis is only a summary; it doesn't show the reader anything new or to be argued.)

3. Junot Diaz is an important American fiction writer. (This is too broad to argue.)

4. Readers should pay close attention to Junot Diaz's uses of dialogue, irony, and language. (Readers can see an interesting thesis here and expect to see support for why the writer chooses to ask the reader to focus on these elements/why they argue we should pay close attention.)

5. Gabriel Garcia Marquez asks his readers to enter a world where the impossible happens. (This is not a thesis yet; we are only reading summary from the writer.)

6. Magical realism is a confusing literary genre. (This is also not a thesis yet; it's vague and doesn't give the reader points it will argue/support.)

7. One can find a connection between Americans' health and nutritional choices. (This thesis is a good start; the reader can expect to see evidence of the connection discussed.)

8. Ohio high school students are being let down by school menu decision makers; their health and academic success remain at stake. (This thesis is stronger on the topic; it's specific on both aspects; who is affected and how they are affected.)

9. College students should take advantage of publication opportunities with The New York Times because of the practical experience, networking opportunities, and resume additions. (This is a great thesis; the writer has set up a claim and will have discussion of three specific reasons.)

10. The New York Times offers writing opportunities to college students. (This is not a thesis yet; it's a summary - if it wanted to argue who offers the best writing opportunities to college students, that would be a better thesis. It could say The New York Times offers writing opportunities to college students which are better than those available at the Lakeland Gazette. Then you could write a compare/contrast essay to support your thesis.)

Exercise 6: Rewrite 1st sentence

On pages 154 and 155 you read about the different ways to write a hook. Some of the options are to use a quotation, a question, a definition, an anecdote, something humorous, song lyrics, a familiar saying, an analogy, or a fact or statistic.

Topic: U.S. veterans and homelessness
Hook:_____

Thesis Statement: _____

Topic: "Thirteen can be an extremely difficult age"
Hook:_____

Thesis Statement: _____

Topic: Online Education
Hook:_____

Thesis Statement: _____

Topic: The future of Amazon
Hook:_____

Thesis Statement: _____

Topic: Birth order and its effect on personality

Hook:_____

Thesis Statement: _____

Developing your introductory paragraph and concluding it with the thesis statement

Your introductory paragraph has three parts: the hook, 2-3 sentences about the topic that connects the hook and the thesis, and the thesis.

The 2-3 sentences give more detail about the topic and lead into the thesis statement. The sentences are placed between the hook and the thesis sentence - think of them as the meat in a sandwich between two pieces of bread (the "hook" and the thesis statement.) This configuration is often called "the sandwich effect!"

Hook and thesis are bread and sentences in the middle are meat.

The last sentence of the introductory paragraph will be the arguable thesis statement.

Example introduction

When I asked my students if they could live for a month without their cell phone and Ipad for a month, there was an overwhelming response - no way, you must be kidding! In this day and age, social media has an enormous impact on our culture, and it is beginning to take over people's lives. Every day when I am walking to class, it is rare to see someone who is not using technology. I attend one of the most beautiful college campuses, and the students are not taking in the scenery. Whether it is listening to music, studying for an exam, or checking Instagram, people are always on their phones. When taking a step back, this reveals a lot about current culture and how technology and social media are becoming driving forces in current culture. **Social media can begin to become addictive and potentially led to isolation because it can consume one and begin to ruin your life.**

This introduction begins with a hook, an anecdote in which a college instructor asks students if they could live for a month without their cell phone and Ipad, the experience would... The hook is followed with sentences that add detail such as walking and observing everyone using their cell phones and ignoring their surroundings. The last sentence is the arguable thesis about how social media can lead to addiction/isolation.

Exercise 7: Complete an introductory paragraph.

The "hook" and thesis statement have been written for you. Complete this paragraph by writing 2-3 sentences in the space between the hook and thesis statement that adds detail and links the "hook" to the thesis statement.

1. *(hook)* The best present I ever received was the Labradoodle I got for my ninth birthday.

_____
_____
_____

(thesis statement) Without a doubt, a dog is a much better pet than a cat and is definitely "man's best friend."

2. *(hook)* When I saw the bruises and her sudden refusal to go to school, I discovered my daughter was a victim of bullying.

_____
_____
_____

(thesis statement) The victims of bullying can have long lasting, lifetime effects.

3. *(hook)* Can you believe that many Canadian cities have an average snowfall of almost 120 inches?

_____
_____
_____

(thesis statement) The reason the Canadians win so many medals at the winter Olympics is because of the weather.

Exercise 8: Putting your Introductory Paragraph together.

In Exercise 6 on page 160, you wrote a "hook" and thesis statement. Use the same "hook" and thesis statement and now write at least 2-3 connecting sentences between the "hook" and thesis statement that add details. It's OK to use the Internet or other source.

Topic: U.S. veterans and homelessness

Hook:_____

Thesis Statement: _____

Topic: "Thirteen can be an extremely difficult age"
Hook:_____

Thesis Statement: _____

Topic: Online Education
Hook:_____

Thesis Statement: _____

Topic: The future of Amazon
Hook:_____

Thesis Statement: _____

Topic: Birth order and its effect on personality
Hook:_____

Thesis Statement: _____

Congratulations! Now you know how to write an introductory paragraph. In Challenge 2 you will learn how to complete your essay with body paragraphs and a conclusion.

CHALLENGE 2
Developing your essay and finishing with a strong conclusion

You have learned that the thesis statement is the main idea of the entire essay and all the paragraphs in the body of the essay will support the thesis. Each body paragraph begins with a topic sentence followed by sentences that have details and examples to support the topic sentence. There is no set number of body paragraphs for your essay nor is there a set length for paragraphs. The number of paragraphs will vary according to the assignment and thesis. Transitional words link the paragraphs so the reader is aware of how the information among paragraphs is related. The final paragraph is the concluding paragraph.

Transition and Vivid Verbs. Two types of words, transition and vivid verbs, will make your readers want to continue reading **and**, using these types of words will make you a much better writer!

Transitional words keep the essay "flowing" so there are no abrupt changes or choppiness among ideas. Comprehension is facilitated because readers become more aware of how information from one sentence to another is related to the next sentence and how ideas and thoughts from paragraph to paragraph is related or connected.

Commonly used transition words. In addition to, furthermore, moreover, besides, also, another, equally important, first, second, etc., further, last, finally, as well as, next, likewise, similarly, in fact, as a result, consequently, for example, for instance, however, therefore, subsequently, although, while it may be true, above all, to enumerate, to explain.

Vivid words are the descriptive words that create a strong, expressive image in the reader's mind.

Common words are replaced with more colorful, exciting, "vivid" words such as "like" can be replaced with "adore," "admire," and "cherish." "Dislike" can be replaced with "loathe, despise, and "scorn."

Exercise 9: The first part of the sentence is written for you.

Add a sentence or phrase to complete sentences 1-12.

1. You might assume that Antarctica is covered with snow year-round, but
_____.

2. I believe that the well-known saying, "Music Soothes the Wild Beast" is valid, however, _____.

3. Of course a high standardized test score is necessary for admittance, but equally important _____.

4. A trip to Asia would be exciting and, furthermore, _____
_____.

5. Although pizza is delicious and is my favorite food, it is, in fact _____
_____.

6. The generals planned the maneuver carefully and, finally _____
_____.

7. I've been in the doldrums since I lost my job and, as a result _____
_____.

8. The college freshman was in such a quandary and didn't know where to turn for help, but _____.

9. Most of the women's club members are matrons, although _____
_____ .

10. Fred was a "perfect" host at the alumni party, however, _____
_____ .

11. I enjoy European foreign films, furthermore _____
_____ .

12. In our city traveling during rush hour is usually horrendous, moreover
_____ .

The Body Paragraphs

You will want at least three body paragraphs although the number depends on the topic and thesis statement. Each body paragraph begins with the topic sentence. Use examples and supporting details to explain and clarify the topic sentences. Have at least three to four sentences for every "body" paragraph.

Now you are ready for the Conclusion

Often readers judge the entire essay based on the conclusion; this is your last chance to show the reader that your essay is important. The conclusion brings closure to the essay - you will want to end with a strong finish - you want to create a lasting impression.

The conclusion should be planned, written, and revised carefully. Before you write it, go back to the introduction and reread the thesis. Restate the thesis in different words or in a different sentence structure and when you are satisfied with your revised thesis, write it in the first sentence of your conclusion. The rest of the paragraph should have two or three sentences that pull ideas together and brings closure to the specific and argumentative thesis that your essay is important. The conclusion brings closure to the essay - you want to end with a strong finish - you want to create a lasting impression.

Conclusion Check-List

👉 Don't repeat any information word-for-word although you can rephrase your points.

👉 A conclusion should answer the question "so what?" It should leave the reader feeling that the information matters - the conclusion should justify the importance of the essay.

👉 Do not add new information to the conclusion; you can synthesize your points and arrive at a new way of looking at something.

👉 Restate the thesis statement in a new way.

👉 Avoid phrases such as *in summary, in conclusion, to conclude.*

👉 The conclusion should leave the reader with the information that matters.

 This is an essay outline to use when planning. Some parts of the outline have been completed. Always try to use some transaction and "vivid words."

Your Introduction

Hook _____

_____

2-3 sentences with illustrations, examples, arguments, and/or facts

_____
_____
_____
_____

Thesis sentence

_____
_____

First Topic Sentence
2-3 sentences with illustrations, examples, arguments, and/or facts

_____
_____
_____
_____

Second Topic Sentence
2-3 sentences with illustrations, examples, arguments, and/or facts

_____
_____

_____

_____

Third Topic Sentence
2-3 sentences with illustrations, examples, arguments, and/or facts

_____

_____

_____

_____

Conclusion _____

_____

Restated thesis statement _____

_____

_____

Let the reader know that the argument has been resolved.

Exercise 10: Below is the Essay Outline. Some parts are complete.

Finish **the introduction** (Write the hook and then write 2-3 sentences between the hook and thesis sentence.)
Body paragraphs (2-3 sentences with illustrations, examples, arguments, facts.)
The conclusion (2-3 sentences of concluding remarks.)

Your Introduction
Hook _____

_____

Thesis sentence
Although helpful and necessary for learning and connecting with friends and family, overuse of technology contributes to problems for college freshmen.

First Topic Sentence
College freshmen should spend more time socializing than on technology.

_____

_____

_____

Second Topic Sentence
Too much technology takes away time that should be spent on homework and classes.

_____

_____

_____

Third Topic Sentence
Studies show that too much technology affects mental and physical health.

_____

_____

_____

Illustrations, examples, arguments, facts

Conclusion
Restate thesis statement _____

_____

_____

Concluding Remarks (let the reader know the argument has been resolved.)

_____

_____

_____

_____

_____

Exercise 11: Writing to learn

In the essay, *Writing to Learn*, the introduction has been written. Read it carefully and complete Paragraphs 1, 2, and 3, by writing at least two more sentences for each paragraph The topic sentences have been written. Your two or three sentences need to support the topic sentence. Then write a conclusion. Make sure to read the Conclusion Check-List before writing the conclusion.

Introduction
When I was in high school I got into trouble with my teacher because I wrote in my textbook - she said this was not allowed! *Naturally, I was so surprised when a college professor I had in my freshman year told us to read with a pencil and write in the book! She said that all books not just workbooks, were meant to be written in. She continued to say that a textbook is*

a "learning tool" and should, over time, look used and worn and not kept in its original condition.

Thesis Statement
If you want a high rate of reading comprehension, always buy a hard copy of your textbook for every class so you can annotate as you read.

Paragraph #1
You can learn a lot by writing in a textbook.

Paragraph #2
A textbook is more expensive than an online text but it's a bargain in the long run.

Paragraph #3
Reviewing chapters for a test is easy because of all the notes, underlining, circling, and stars you made with your pen, pencil, and colored markers.

Conclusion
A word about essay exams:
Students generally prefer essay exams over multiple choice exams because they have the flexibility and the chance to put into words what they know and what they have learned. Essay questions are graded on the content and how well it is explained. Taking a few minutes to make sure the essay question is understood and to know exactly what the essay question is really asking is very important. It's wise to jot down the facts and ideas that accurately answers the question before "jumping in" to answer the question.

An essay exam puts you in control. Instead of choosing answers as you do in a multiple choice exam, you can recall and organize ideas and facts and plan how to express them in a thoughtful, systematic way.

Now you are a better writer.

Chapter Summary

You've gained skills with thesis writing, introductions, topic sentences, transitions, body paragraphs, and conclusions. Now that you've learned these building blocks with college essay assignments, you are ready to learn more about succeeding with writing in all types of courses.

Flower: The Strategy for Essay Exams

"If you only read the books that everyone else is reading, you can only think what everyone else is thinking."

Haruki Murakami

Course: All courses that have essay exams

Goal: To prepare for essay exams

Material Needed: List of essay prompt words, textbook, handouts, class notes and other material needed to prepare for exam, paper, pen and pencil

Individual or group: Individual

Lesson Duration: Approximately four – six hours total

Finished Product to be graded: Written answers to essay questions to be graded

Why do I need to learn this?

If you are going to have an essay exam, you should prepare for the exam by writing answers to possible essay questions. Studying for essay exams is different from studying for multiple choice exams.

Procedure

Step 1 and 2:   **F** *Formulate* essay questions with your *list* of question words and a

                    L *List* of all the topics you think will be on the text

Step 3:   **O** *Organize and outline* all the facts and details that will answer each question you made.

Step 4:   **W** *Write answer to each question.*

                    E *Evaluate* look at your notes to make sure you have included the pertinent facts and details.

Step 5:   **R** *Rewrite* up your answer and write from memory.

Final Thoughts

Too many students prepare for a test by reading and rereading their notes over and over. The FLOWER strategy is an active strategy because you have to predict questions and then write the answers. Remember, we maximize learning when we *Write about it.*

Question words for essay exam

Analyze	Break into separate parts and discuss, examine, or interpret each part.
Compare	Examine two or more things, identify similarities and difference.
Contrast	Show differences
Criticize	Make judgments of good points and limitations, with evidence.
Define	Give the meaning, but no details.
Describe	Give a detailed account. List characteristics and qualities.
Discuss	Give pro and con reasons with details.
Enumerate	List the points.
Evaluate	Discuss advantages and disadvantages with your opinion.
Explain	Give reasons for happenings or events.
Illustrate	Give concrete examples. Explain clearly by using comparisons or examples.
Interpret	State the meaning in simpler terms, using your judgment.
Outline	Make a short summary with headings and subheadings.
Prove	Give evidence and reasons supported with facts.
Relate	Show how two or more things are connected.
State	List the main points briefly without details.
Summarize	Give a brief, condensed account and avoid unnecessary details.
Trace	Give main points from beginning to end of an event.

7

Writing to Learn
in the Content Areas

A tearful Nancy bravely called her teacher and made an appointment to see her. The following is an interaction Nancy had with her advisor.

Nancy: "Please help me! I have failed two tests in your class, and if I fail another, then I'll fail your class."

Teacher: "Now let's settle down and take a look at the two tests you failed."

After three minutes go by.....

Teacher: "Yes, I had to give you a failing mark on both of these exams but I think I figured out why you failed them. Now before I do that I would like to know how you studied for these tests."

Nancy: "I'm a pretty good note-taker so I studied and reviewed my notes until I practically had them memorized. I knew everything so why did I fail the exam?"

Teacher: To me the answer is obvious. All the questions you missed were from the assigned chapters I told you to read. Obviously, you didn't read them."

Nancy: I guess you're right but the chapters are so boring!!

Teacher: I thought you liked reading.

Readers and Writers
Are Interesting

Have acquired a lot of knowledge and ideas

Are curious

Are open-minded to new ideas

Are empathetic toward others

Like their own company

Have good imaginations

Have patience

Are good observers

Like learning new things

Nancy: "Yes, but I love to read novels and stories but, most of all, I love writing my own stories. I've been doing this for years."

Teacher: "Ummmmm - I have a great idea. Have you heard of the Write to Learn Strategy? It's a no-brainer. I think you'll like it."

Nancy: "OK—I'm listening."

Teacher: "First, start reading your assignment for ten minutes. Then stop, close the book, and write for 4 minutes about what you just read. If you can't remember what you just read, that is a wake-up call letting you know you'd better read it again. By the way, you can do this strategy in any class such as biology, history, or psychology."

Nancy: "I think I'll try it."

Teacher: "This strategy makes it easy to learn…you'll have your textbook notes to review. I almost forgot to tell you that after you have written your first summary, resume reading for ten minutes and write your next summary. If you do this for at least 50-60 minutes a day about 4-5 times a week. I guarantee that your reading comprehension and reading rate will improve."

Nancy: "I think I'll try it. I think this is a "win-win" situation - I think I'll become a better reader and writer at the same time - and I think this strategy is going to help stay in school and graduate!"

In this chapter you will read about:

Reading and Writing

Writing Activities

Exercises 1-12

CHALLENGE 1
Using writing to promote learning in content areas

Some interesting points about reading and writing

Writers and authors strongly believe that a strong foundation in reading is needed to become a skillful writer. The best advice for someone wanting a career in journalism, law, advertising, screen writing, speech writing, copy editing, social media, writing lyrics, writing novels, technology, writing biographies, or marketing is to read the works of quality, respected writers.

Listening to books on tape is almost as good as reading because you will be able to hear the way accomplished writers use language patterns and words.

One of the best ways to learn and remember information is to combine reading with writing.

Writing to promote learning in content areas is not new - but it is evident that writing about it is what we need to do after we read. But, before we begin to write, we need to do something else. We need to think about what we just read. Continuous reading, without pausing to think and reflect, affects comprehension. Furthermore, it often creates "mindless reading." Teachers seldom remind students that pausing after reading a paragraph or two and thinking about what was just read can dramatically improve comprehension. And, if students write about what was read after thinking, the results would become even more dramatic.

The valuable message of this chapter is that our readers will include writing with reading assignments.

Remember.. Reading is Thinking!

Competency in writing develops over time

CHALLENGE 2
Writing activities for content areas

Writing activities to increase learning

Informal and formal writing are the two kinds of writing in higher education. Informal writing is usually brief, done quickly, and often impromptu. Content is important; form and style are not. Some examples of informal writing are summaries, journals, freewriting, note-taking, emails, texting, social media posts, and blogging. Formal writing is the kind of writing that goes from the draft stage to the well written, final product and demonstrates knowledge about a particular subject. Examples of formal writing are scholarly papers, research reports, essays, term papers, and essay exams.

Students can learn more and retain more when they combine writing with their textbook reading assignments. An easy way to do this is to read with a pencil. Lucy Calkins (1986) says that when reading, a student should also be "Thinking with A Pencil in Hand." Thinking about reading and putting those thoughts in your own words on paper is a strategy that students can do in every class. It becomes even more powerful when the student connects the new information with his/her prior knowledge base.

Accomplished writers learn their craft from reading what other respected, well-regarded writers have written. The New York Times, Washington Post, The Economist, and scholarly journals are just a few sources that emulate good models of writing. We urge students to read quality periodicals. Soon they will begin to notice the vocabulary, language style, and sentence construction that skillful writers use to strengthen their writing skills.

The easiest (and perhaps the best way) to combine reading with writing is to write summaries. A summary shows your understanding of information and ideas. It briefly restates in your own words, the content, the central idea, and main points. A summary can contain the answers to "who, what, where, when, why, and how."

Exercise 1: Write an informative paragraph explaining the following quotes.

"Everyone thinks of changing the world, but no one thinks of changing himself."

Leo Tolstoy

"What we learn in childhood is carved in stone. What we learn as adults is carved in ice."

David Kherdian

"Computers are incredibly fast, accurate, and stupid; Humans are incredibly slow, inaccurate and brilliant; Together they are powerful beyond imagination."

Albert Einstein

"A child only educated at school is an uneducated child."

George Santayana

"It is the mark of an educated mind to be able to entertain a thought without accepting it."

Aristotle

"If you don't have the time to read, you won't have the time to write."

Stephen King

Exercise 2: An idiom is a figurative expression that does not have a correct literal meaning. Instead it has an implied meaning. Explain the meaning of each idiom and give an example for each one.

Dog eat dog

Head and shoulders above

Hit pay dirt

Rolling in the aisles

Exercise 3: From a Developmental Reading Course

Read the following paragraph and in your opinion, write a 2-3 sentence summary that suggests ways to keep high school students from being dropouts.

Educators, especially reading specialists, say that the more you read, the more you know and the less you read the less you know. They also cite the statistics which say that 70 to 82% of prison inmates are school dropouts. Furthermore, they say that the more diplomas one has the longer that person will live and the more money that person will make! Try to include some of your own suggestions.

Exercise 4: From a Geography textbook

Read the paragraph and then finish the letter that a teenager is writing to his mom about visiting Lake Bled. Use at least 100 more words. It's OK to add more details.

Lake Bled, one of the ten most beautiful lakes in the world is located in Slovenia, and is nestled among the Julian Alps and Karavanda Mountains. Most people have a vague idea where Slovenia is, let alone the location of Lake Bled. Although one would expect Lake Bled to be very chilly, it is relatively warm because the mountains shield it from the icy northern winds. The lake surrounds bled Island where tourists are beginning to flock to visit a 15th century church, a popular place for weddings. After making the list of the ten most beautiful lakes in the world, Lake Bled will probably never be the same.

Dear Mom,
I am a wonderful time in Lake Bled.

_____
_____
_____
_____
_____
_____
_____
_____
_____
_____
_____
_____

Exercise 5: From a Freshman Success class

Listed below is a list of characteristics of successful students. You have been asked to write an article for the college newspaper, "Become A Successful Student." Make sure you have a "hook" and write a minimum of 120 words.

1. Successful students are responsible for every outcome - both the good and the bad.

2. They never see themselves as victims.

3. They have realistic goals and dreams.

4. They consistently plan and take action in the pursuit of their goals.

5. They avoid procrastination.

6. Throughout the years, they keep relationships with people who have been instrumental in helping them.

7. They seek advice when needed.

8. They enjoy learning outside of classes because they have a curiosity that enriches their lives.

9. They have a healthy, positive outlook on life and have the emotional maturity to cope with the "ups and downs" of life.

10. They can delay gratification.

11. They view themselves a worthy, capable people and communicate this trait to others.

Exercise 6: From a newspaper

Decide whether a parent should get a dog or cat for their nine year old child. Then write a persuasive paragraph that expresses your views about whether parents should get a dog or cat for their child.

Dogs have more stamina than cats. Huskies or sled dogs can run 1,000 miles in two weeks and burn as many as 12,000 calories a day. Cats, however, are more agile. They live up to the expression, "they always land on their feet" when falling from several stories. Although both dogs and cats hunt, cats are considered the better hunter. Some estimate they kill between 1.4 and 3.7 billion birds each year. Dogs are more hardworking than cats. Unlike felines, they can be trained as guide dogs, herd dogs, and detection dogs for illicit drugs and criminals. Dogs also have a better sense of smell, run faster than cats, and are considered smarter of the two species. Cats, however, have a longer life span and are more independent.

Exercise 7: From a horticulture class

There are 10 sentences listed below. Use the sentences to write 2-3 paragraphs. Begin each paragraph with a topic sentence and will regroup the sentences according to the topic sentence. You may want to combine sentences with transition words - just make sure to include all the facts in the ten sentences.

1. The beautiful red and green plants associated with Christmas are usually holly and poinsettias.

2. The red berries found on holly represent the blood of Christ, especially when they were made into wreaths to represent Christ's Crown of Thorns.

3. The poinsettia was brought to the US from Mexico by Dr. Joel Poinsett in 1825.

4. Poinsett was appointed US Ambassador to Mexico by President John Quincy Adams.

5. Because Poinsett was interested in plants, he brought the American elm to Mexico.

6. While in Mexico, he found a shrub alongside the road which had very large red flowers.

7. He took cuttings to his greenhouse in South Carolina.

8. It is estimated that this bright red and green plant with star-shaped leaves outsells other potted plants by 15 to 1 during the Christmas season.

9. Today poinsettias come in all shades of red, pink, and white.

10. Next Christmas when you see a poinsettia, you may start to wonder if that plant's ancestors came from Dr. Poinsett's cuttings.

Exercise 8: From a marketing textbook

After you read this paragraph, write the answer to this question: "In your opinion what is the future of board games?" Include in your remarks the impact that video games have on young people. Use 250 – 3000 words.

Charles Darrow, a US heating engineer, invented the board game Monopoly in 1935. He sought to improve on the basic idea that Elizabeth Phillips had in 1924. At that time the US was going through The Great Depression and the game gave people a chance to feel rich and powerful. The names of the streets in the game were from Atlantic City, New Jersey, a favorite vacation place. He fashioned the tokens from his wife's charm bracelet. One year later, there was a British version of Monopoly which had London street names. Monopoly is the world's number one board game and is sold in 103 countries and translated into thirty-seven languages. There are some interesting facts about Monopoly. When Fidel Castro took power in Cuba, he ordered all Monopoly games destroyed. The three most landed on properties are Illinois Avenue, "GO", and the B & O Railroad. There have been 250 million Monopoly games sold. The total amount of money in one game of Monopoly is $15,140.

Exercise 9: From an English composition class

Your instructor has asked you to write a 125-150 word summary based on the following article about writing. The title of your summary is: "How to Become a Good Writer."

Becoming a good writer doesn't happen overnight. In most cases it takes years of effort and practice. Even though someone may speak English well, this does not necessarily mean that person will write well. There is some interesting advice from recognized writers. Mark Twain said "When you catch adjectives, kill most of them. Then the rest will be valuable. They weaken when they are close together, they give strength when they are far apart." The novelist, John Gardner, said "The abstract is seldom as effective as the concrete. 'She was distressed' is not as good as 'she looked away.'" John Barzun said, "Look for all fancy workings and get rid of them." William Strunk, Jr. wrote, "Vigorous writing is concise." A sentence should contain no unnecessary words and paragraphs, no unnecessary sentences.' The last bit of advice is from Marvin Olasky, an English teacher who wrote, "The way not to learn is to assume that friends who say, 'You're great' have honesty." Young writers need true friends, teachers and editors who are willing to make them cry. All are hard to find in this age of emphasizing self-esteem rather than tough honesty.

Exercise 10: From a biology class

In a short summary (30-50 words) define what is meant by a "collection of compromises."

Biologists, anthropologists, paleontologists, and geneticists see today's human body as a "collection of compromises" as our ancestors have adapted to their environment over time. In an article "Obesity? Big Feet? Blame Darwin" in the Wall Street Journal on 2/22/2010, author Melinda Beck says that some changes have led to modern day maladies. Since the immune system of today does not need to fight malaria and cholera because of cleaner environments, it instead "starts picking fights" with other areas of the body and we are now seeing more asthma and autoimmune disease. Other changes in the past 20,000 years are that jaws have shrunk faster than teeth which have made overcrowding common. The gene for coarse hair is spreading to Asia and the cause is not known. Although the big toe which was common in mountain climbers has shrunk, men and women's feet size in the past 100 years has increased four sizes. In 1900, Americans were the tallest people but that statistic is being challenged by the Europeans and Japanese. In Holland men average over six feet tall and in Japan, which had short people in 1950, now reports that the new population has grown at least five inches.

Exercise 11: From a Government class

Read the following paragraph about Woodrow Wilson and complete the outline at the end of this article. Then use the outline to write 3 short paragraphs which include the details from the article.

Woodrow Wilson was the 28th president of the United States and served two terms. Harry S. Truman in an essay said that there were three presidents who served as his models. Two were Thomas Jefferson and Andrew Jackson, and the third was Woodrow Wilson. When asked to describe Woodrow Wilson, Truman replied, "I guess the best way to describe Wilson if I've got to use a label, is to say he was a commonsense liberal… He was a genuine liberal who used his heart and his brain." Wilson was an intellectual who graduated from Princeton University for his undergraduate degree, from University of Virginia with his law degree, and John Hopkins for his Ph.D. He was a professor at Bryn Mawr from 1885 – 1888 and at Wesleyan University from 1889 – 1890. Later he became President of Princeton University from 1902 – 1910 and governor of New Jersey 1911 – 1913. He served as a Democratic President from

1912 until 1920. Wilson's accomplishments as president were that he established the Federal Reserve Board, the Federal Trade Commission, Anti-Clayton Trust Act, the League of Nations which would later become the United Nations. He won the Nobel Peace Prize as a result of his service to the United Nations.

Main Idea
Woodrow Wilson was the 28th president of the United States.

Major Detail
Harry S. Truman selected Woodrow Wilson as one of his models because of these traits:

a._____

b._____

Woodrow Wilson did many things before becoming President

a._____

b._____

c._____

d._____

Woodrow Wilson's accomplishments as President

a._____

b._____

c._____

d._____

Exercise 12: From a Political Science class

Read the Introduction and the Gettysburg Address and then answer the following questions.

Introduction
The Gettysburg Address was delivered by President Abraham Lincoln on November 19, 1863 at Gettysburg, Pennsylvania. At this time our nation was engaged in the Civil War and Lincoln came to Gettysburg to dedicate the Battle of Gettysburg as a National Cemetery. President Lincoln gave this two minute speech after the main speaker, Edward Everett, spoke for two hours. Many people were surprised that Lincoln's speech was so short and, in fact, Lincoln called it a "flat failure."

The Gettysburg Address
Four score and seven years ago our fathers brought forth on this continent, a new nation, conceived in liberty, and dedicated to the proposition that all men are created equal.

Now we are engaged in a great civil war, testing whether that nation, or any nation so conceived and so dedicated, can long endure. We are met on a great battlefield of that war. We have come to dedicate a portion of that field, as a final resting place for those who here gave their lives that that nation might live. It is altogether fitting and proper that we should do this.

But, in a larger sense, we cannot dedicate - we cannot consecrate - we cannot hallow - this ground. The brave men, living and dead, who struggle here, have consecrated it, far above our poor power to add or detract. The world will little note, nor long remember what we say here, but it can never forget what they did here. It is for us the living, rather, to be dedicated here to the unfinished work which they who fought here have thus far so nobly advanced. It is rather for us to be here dedicated to the great task remaining before us - that from these honored dead we take increased devotion to that cause for which they gave the last full measure of devotion - that we here highly resolve that these dead shall not have died in vain - that this nation, under God, shall have a new birth of freedom - and that government of the people, by the people, for the people, shall not perish from the earth.

1. Is this speech more political or religious? Explain.

2. Lincoln's speech reveals his feelings about a nation at war. How does this speech affect you emotionally?

3. If our current President of the United States were giving a speech to honor our soldiers, what else do you think he/she might include?

4. Lincoln ended his speech with "government of the people, by the people, and for the people." Does that statement still apply today? Why or why not?

5. Veteran's Day is a day to honor our soldiers. Why are people of today less observant of Veteran's Day than they were in the past?

6. What burden(s) is Lincoln placing on the U.S. citizens?

7. Lincoln said our nation was dedicated to the proposition that "all men are created equal." Discuss your viewpoint of this proposition.

Analyzing how correct and incorrect essay prompts are asked on standardized test

Correct options: written that include main idea, major and minor supporting details, facts, and a general sense what the writing is about.

Incorrect options: written response that does not include all of the above.

Chapter Summary

Writing a summary or response to a reading assignment is highly recommended when you need a high level of comprehension. Two reasons for this are (1) in order to write about something, a person must understand what was read and (2) the writer will have the written copy from which to study.

WIMMS Strategy: Writing in Margins Makes Sense

"In the case of a good book, the point is not to see how many of them you can get through, but rather how many can get through to you."

Mortimer Adler

Course: All courses

Goal: To learn textbook information

Material Needed: Textbook, pencil or pen

Individual or group: Individual

Lesson Duration: 45 minute sessions

Finished Product to be graded: Marginal notes in textbook to be graded

Why do I need to learn this?

Throughout your college career you will be asked to respond to assigned reading material. Now is the time to practice and make sure you can write an excellent response.

Procedure

1. Select the pages in the textbook for your upcoming test.

2. Using a pencil or pen, read a paragraph and circle, underline, star, or use some other mark to indicate important information.

3. As you read the paragraph, try to identify the topic sentence.

4. Write the main idea of the paragraph in the margin.

5. Now write a paragraph using your notes on everything you marked.

6. When reviewing for the test, read your marginal notes and anything else you marked in the paragraph.

7. Reread the paragraph if necessary.

8. Continue the next paragraphs by repeating steps 1-6.

Final Thoughts

You will find it is very efficient (and also a timesaver) to have your notes right next to the textbook information. Remember to write in your textbook - don't worry about keeping it in perfect condition in the hopes of selling it for a high price. Receiving an A in a course and low price is so much better than getting a C and a high price!

8

Applying Reading and Writing Connections with Patterns of Organization

Warren Buffet is one of the wealthiest men in the United States. When asked about his "keys to success," Warren Buffet pointed to a stack of books and said,

"Read 500 pages like this every day. That's how knowledge works. It builds up like compound interest. All of you can do it, but I guarantee not many of you will do it."

"Don't forget - no one else sees the world the way you do, so no one else can tell the stories that you have to tell."

Charles deLint

"If you want to be a writer, you must do two things above all others: Read a lot and write a lot."

Stephen King

"A writer only begins a book. A reader finishes it."

Samuel Johnson

"How do I know what I think until I see what I say."

E. M. Forster

In this chapter you will read about:

Learning All About Patterns of Organization

The Ten Basic Patterns of Organization with their related transitional/Signal Words

Examples of Patterns of Organization

How Pattern of Organization Questions are asked on Standardized Tests

Analyzing how Correct and Incorrect Pattern of Organization Questions are worded on Standardized Tests

Strategy: Expository to Narrative

Patterns are everywhere

Here are some conversation

<u>Conversation between an air traffic controller and an airline pilot</u>
Air traffic controller, "Tonight's **weather pattern** shows a thunderstorm will be here by 5:00 am."

Pilot, "I'm glad you warned me because I will definitely have to change my **flight pattern.**"

<u>Conversation between a dress manufacturer and a buyer for a department store</u>
Dress manufacturer, "The **pattern** from Paris with the empire waistline should be my best selling dress this spring."

Department store buyer, "I'll be buying a lot of those, but my **buying pattern** has changed. I now buy fewer petites and more plus sizes."

<u>Conversation between three English instructors</u>
8th grade instructor, "I'm still teaching the traditional **sentence pattern** of noun, verb, and subject."

High school instructor, "I teach the five paragraph **essay pattern** every fall."

College instructor, "I teach my students about the author's **patterns of organization.**"

<u>Conversation between a road builder and a city planner</u>
Road builder, "The **traffic pattern** will improve now that we plan to build roundabouts."

City Planner, "I hope you build according to the **roundabout patterns** used throughout Europe."

<u>Conversation between the city manager and mayor</u>
City manager, "The **demographic pattern** of our city has changed since the last election."

Mayor, "Yes. This has caused the **voting pattern** to change and I'm worried that it will impact my upcoming election."

Do you see that "patterns" can be found everywhere and that there are all kinds of patterns? All these examples show that a pattern is a form or structure to be followed to achieve an end result. Authors use "Patterns of Organization" to organize information to help student's reading comprehension.

Introduction

Information that is arranged in a systematic, orderly way facilitates understanding whereas information that is randomly or haphazardly put together will hinder understanding and most likely cause confusion. Fortunately, most textbook writers are skillful at getting their information understood in a logical, comprehensible way. They do this by using a variety of patterns of organization for their different topics.

Textbook writers choose a pattern of organization that will help the reader understand and remember how the details "fit in" or are arranged in the "big picture." The choice of the pattern used is clearly the writer's decision. There is no rule for which pattern to use. Here is an example. If a writer were asked to write about Central Park in New York City, one writer may choose a Description Pattern. Another writer may choose a Time Order Pattern and yet another writer may use a Summary Pattern. Incidentally, you may already be familiar with Patterns of Organization because they are the same ones you learned in your English composition class when you learned how to plan and organize your essays.

This chapter will familiarize you with ten Patterns of Organization generally found in college level textbooks.

Learning all about Patterns of Organization

"Anyone can be a writer but some writers convey thoughts and ideas better than others."

J. Lopate

CHALLENGE 1
Writing a strong introductory essay paragraph

A textbook writer decides how to organize the information to be presented. In most cases, a topic and the accompanying details could be explained in a number of ways. Suppose a writer's topic was boxing.

Writer A may use a Time-Order Pattern of Organization in which the history of boxing, from ancient Greek and Roman times to present day is explained.

Writer B may use a Cause-Effect Pattern of Organization which shows the effects that boxing has on individuals who participate in the sport.

Writer C may use a Description Pattern which describes the different levels of boxing, the training to become a boxer, and the techniques of boxing.

Writer D may use a Summary Pattern which includes condensed version of the main aspects of boxing.

Transitional or signal words are the key important words to look for with Patterns of Organization. Be aware of these words during reading because they provide clues that signal which Pattern of Organization is being used. They also connect or relate ideas within or between sentences. For instance, if a friend said, "My car was broken into and the thieves stole my computer, wallet, and luggage," you might predict that if the next word were "and" you would be expecting more bad news. If, however, the next word was "but," you would probably expect something more positive to occur: "My car was broken into and the thieves stole my computer, wallet, and luggage, **but** the police came immediately and recovered everything!"

Example #1: Here are two sentences. Notice that they don't seem related or connected.

> I bought beautiful living room furniture from an online store. The furniture is larger than I realized, and it looks terrible in the room.

Example #2: Here are the same sentences, slightly revised. Can you see the big difference?

> I bought beautiful living room furniture from an online store; **however,** the furniture is larger than I realized and it looks terrible in the room!

The signal/transition word "however" has been added to link the two sentences. Notice the sentences are now connected and your understanding has improved.

Table 1 shows ten common patterns of organization and their signal or transition words. It is important to learn the transitional/signal words associated with each pattern.

"Just write every day of your life. Read intensely. Then see what happens. Most of my friends who are put on that diet have very pleasant careers."
Ray Bradbury

Table 1

The ten basic patterns of organization with their related transitional/signal words

Patterns of Organization	Signal/Transition Words
Patterns that catalog information	
Topic List	in addition, several, also, another, a number of, several, few, many
Time-Order	stages, steps, previously, first, second, third, until, at last, before, after, next, when, later, following
Spatial/Place	above, over, under, nearby, around, next to, beside, inside, below, behind, outside, in front of, behind
Summary	finally, in brief, overall, hence, to conclude, in summary
Patterns that describe, show, or illustrate	
Example/Illustrate	specifically, for example, that is, for instance, such as, to demonstrate, to illustrate, including, to show
Definition	is defined as, is called, means, refers to, a term, concept, to describe, features
Description	to describe, features
Patterns that give information	
Division/Classification	aspects, properties, divided into, groups, parts, categories, elements, types, features, characteristics, divisions, kinds
Cause-Effect	since, thus, as a result, because, consequently, therefore, hence, due to, accordingly
Comparison/Contrast	as well as, similar, different, than, instead, however, parallels, on the other hand, but, in the same way

Types of patterns of organization

The Topic-List pattern is used for topics having a group of items or ideas which are then discussed one item at a time. The order of the items is not important, items can be randomly discussed.

Aristophanes, Euripides, Socrates, Plato, and Aristotle are several of the ancient Greek philosophers who are widely read today.

Topic List

The Definition pattern defines specialized vocabulary, ideas, terms, and concepts from specific academic areas. Definitions are clarified with examples and restatements.

The meaning of xenophobia is an unreasonable fear, distrust, or hatred of strangers, foreigners, or anything that is different from the person's perspective or surroundings.

Definition

The Division or Classification pattern is used with topics or concepts which have several categories or parts. Information is divided into groups, and then each one is explained.

The endocrine system is composed of glands which secrete hormones to control functions of cells, tissues, and organs. The endocrine system includes the adrenal glands, parathyroid glands, pituitary gland, and thyroid as well as the ovaries, pancreas, and testes.

Division/ Classification

The Compare/Contrast pattern shows the similarities and differences between two things. The Comparison pattern points out how things are similar; the Contrast pattern points out how things are different.

A Type A personality is someone who is competitive, ambitious, has a high need to achieve, and who can be controlling whereas a Type B personality is someone who is relaxed and noncompetitive.

Compare/ Contrast

The Cause-Effect pattern is used to show that something happened which caused an effect on something else. This pattern usually involves the how, why, consequences, and results.

The Great Depression which began in 1929 and lasted until the start of World War II caused poverty, unemployment, falling prices, and lower business and trade.

Cause-Effect

The Example/Illustrate pattern explains an idea or concept through examples. Examples, especially those that students are familiar with, clarify and/or illustrate the new concept.

An example of a country with an almost zero population growth will be China by the year 2030.

Example/Illustrate

The Spatial pattern identifies the location, arrangement, or whereabouts of an object or how they go together. The spatial pattern, like the description pattern, helps the reader transform words into a visual representation

Route 66, also known as "The Mother Road," stretches 2448 miles from Chicago, Illinois to Santa Monica, California. It passes through eight states and also through St. Louis, MO; Tulsa, OK; Oklahoma City, OK; Amarillo, TX; Albuquerque, NM; Flagstaff, AZ; Kingman, AZ and Barstow, CA until it ends in Santa Monica, CA.

Spatial/Place

The Description pattern describes or illustrates the characteristics of a person, place, or thing. This helps students visualize what is being described.

Mount Rushmore, a mountain in the Black Hills, is two miles from Rapid City, South Dakota. There, busts of four U.S. presidents are carved into the 5,725 foot granite mountain. The presidents are George Washington, Thomas Jefferson, Theodore Roosevelt, and Abraham Lincoln. Each head is 60 feet tall which is the equivalent of a six-story building. Their noses are 20 feet long, each mouth is 18 feet wide, and the eyes are 11 feet across.

Description

The Time-Order pattern, often called the Chronological pattern, presents items in a sequence, chronological order, or in the order in which they appeared.

Jackie Robinson, one of baseball's greatest player was born in 1919 Cairo, Georgia. As a black athlete, he faced discrimination when he joined the Brooklyn Dodgers in 1947. Two years later, he was voted Rookie of the Year. In 1949 he was the National League's Most Valuable Player. From 1949 until 1954 he was selected for six consecutive years to the All Star Game. He was inducted into the Baseball Hall of Fame in 1962 at the age of 53.

Time-Order

The Summary pattern condenses major points and the significant details into a brief version of the original piece

In a brief summary, Madam Marie Curie was a French chemist of Polish descent who, with her husband, Pierre Curie, discovered radium.

Summary

CHALLENGE 2
How to increase learning with patterns of organization

Meeting the challenge

At this point, you may be wondering why is it important to identify Patterns of Organization. Processing information is easier when you understand the way the author arranged or organized the main ideas and details. Furthermore, comprehension will improve because you are thinking in the same way as the author. By recognizing the Pattern of Organization, you will become a more active, involved listener because you are now able to anticipate the forthcoming information. The next time you have a reading assignment or listen to a lecture, try to recognize the Pattern of Organization used.

Can there be more than one Pattern of Organization in a paragraph? In most cases, one Pattern of Organization is used for a paragraph; however, there can be more than one Pattern of Organization or a mix of patterns in a paragraph.

What can I do to find the pattern of organization?
Begin reading the paragraph to find the pattern of organization because the paragraph often comprises the basic unit of thought. The topic sentence may provide clues as to how the paragraph or the overall passage is organized. Identifying the signal words also provide clues to the organization. Review the information provided in Challenge 1 of this chapter, which explains and gives examples of Patterns of Organization and the associated transitional/signal words.

"This is how you do it. You sit down at a keyboard and you put one word after another until it's done. It's that easy, and that hard."

Neil Guiman

How patterns of organization questions are asked on standarized tests

1. In this paragraph/passage, the author uses an organizational pattern of...

2. Which of the choices below demonstrates an organizational pattern used in the paragraph/passage?

3. The primary organizational pattern is…..

4. Which of the choices below demonstrates the organizational pattern the author used to present his/her idea?

 ## Analyzing how correct and incorrect pattern of organization questions are worded on standardized tests.

Correct Options

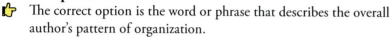 The correct option is the word or phrase that describes the overall author's pattern of organization.

Incorrect Options

👉 An option that depicts a minor pattern of organization in the passage and not the overall pattern of organization.

👉 An *option* that depends on the clue word alone and does not take into consideration the overall pattern which may not have a clue word.

👉 An option that reflects the organizational pattern of one sentence and not the overall pattern.

👉 A pattern that reflects an organizational pattern that does not appear in the passage.

 ## Exercise 1: Read each sentence and choose the pattern of organization.

1. A psychology professor is lecturing about four branches of psychology not in any particular order.
a. Topic List   b. Time Order   c. Cause-Effect

2. An economics professor is lecturing about ways franchises are different from private owned companies.
a. Topic List   b. Summary   c. Compare-Contrast

3. A geography professor is lecturing about how continents evolved millions of years ago and their effect on land formation today.
a. Definition   b. Classification   c. Cause-Effect

4. A religion professor discusses the features or components of the Hindu religion.
a. Classification   b. Spatial   c. Cause-Effect

5. A genetics professor explains the differences in the ways dominant and recessive traits are passed on.
a. spatial   b. Topic List   c. Compare-Contrast

6. An education professor discusses word identification in primary grades and then chooses four main methods of word identification and discusses each in depth.
a. Classification   b. Spatial   c. Cause-Effect

7. An anthropology professor traces the development of tools used by Neanderthal man to modern man.
a. Time Order   b. Definition   c. Summary

8. A history professor spoke about how the Coliseum, Pantheon, Appian Way, and the Forum were situated right near modern buildings in Rome.
a. Spatial   b. Topic List   c. Definition

9. An English professor read three of O'Henry's short stories.
a. Definition   b. Topic-List   c. Summary

10. A biology professor highlights all of Charles Darwin's theories in one class session.
a. Cause-Effect   b. Definition   c. Summary

11. A sociology professor spoke about acculturation and what it means in different cultures.
a. Definition   b. Time Order   c. Classification

12. An art history professor showed several well- known paintings from the Baroque Period.
a. Summary   b. Example/Illustration   c. Definition

13. A sports administrator professor lectures that the revenue from all football games provides revenue for some of the other sports at the university.
a. Cause-Effect   b. Compare-Contrast   c. Definition

14. A political science professor describes the concept of "cruel and unusual punishment."

a. Spatial   b. Definition   c. Topic List

15. A music professor tells the class how the first production of Porgy and Bess differs from the most recent production on Broadway.

a. Spatial   b. Classification   c. Compare-Contrast

Exercise 2: Choose the pattern of organization for each sentence.

Topic List | Description | Compare | Contrast | Example/Illustrate

1. A baseball sportswriter is going to write about the differences between the American and National Leagues. _____

2. A geography professor lectured how water in the Dead Sea was like water in the Indian Ocean. _____

3. A coin buyer advertised in the local papers that he was interested in buying Buffalo nickels, mercury dimes, wheat pennies, and Morgan dollars. _____

4. The fashion designer held up a sketch and told the head seamstress the dress needed to be exactly like the one in the sketch. She insisted a copy of the sketch be placed at each cutting table and sewing machine.

_____

5. I asked her to tell me all the details about her new job as president of production. _____

Cause-Effect | Time-Order | Summary | Classification | Definition

1. He called her brother obtuse but no one in the family knew the meaning--that this was an insulting term for slow witted people.

_____

2. I am always the first one to my early class. The first thing I do is to take out my agenda and write my "to do list" for the day, then have my first cup of coffee, go to all my classes and end this perfect day by reading my novel in bed. _____

3. Because the price of buying gas for her daily 70 mile round trip was steadily going up and she could no longer afford the fuel, she decided to

buy a "smart car." _____

4. The jeweler said my budget would determine the type of gold necklace I could afford. He said gold comes in 3 grades: 10K, gold filled, 14K, or 18k . _____

5. On my last English essay test I had to write an overview or main points of the short story. _____

Exercise 3: Select two patterns of organization for each paragraph.

1. The reading teacher gave an entire lecture about skimming. Altogether, she presented six situations when skimming would be useful. Then she followed up with examples how to with different types of reading material.
    a. Description and Example
    b. Definition and Time-Order
    c. Description and Spatial

2. Our art teacher showed an impressionistic still life painting and then a realistic still life painting so we could understand the similarities and differences. Then she created her own still life arrangement by placing real objects next to, behind, in front of each other so her arrangement became a still life for us to draw.
    a. Time-Order and Cause-Effect
    b. Definition and Time-Order
    c. Compare-Contrast and Spatial

3. In a health class several communicative diseases were discussed: small pox, influenza, and measles. The professor made this very interesting by tell us the impact the European explorers made on the Native Americans who had no immunity to the germs brought from Europe.
    a. Time-Order and Spatial
    b. Cause-Effect and Contrast
    c. Classification and Cause-Effect

4. Wolfgang Amadeus Mozart was a classical music prodigy. He was born in 1756 and by age six composed minuets, played the piano and wrote fugues. At eight years he wrote a symphony, at age eleven he wrote an oratorio, and at age twelve wrote an opera all of which will be described in detail.
    a. Time-Order and Spatial
    b. Time-Order and Description
    c. Compare-Contrast and Time-Order

5. My religion professor lectured about the three branches of Judaism and gave a brief synopsis of each one.
    a. Compare-Contrast and Spatial
    b. Classification and Description
    c. Cause-Effect and Example

Exercise 4: From an architecture class

Read paragraphs 1 and 2 which are about an architect who is going to design a new house for his cousin. You are to finish writing paragraphs 3-8 using the specified pattern of organization.
• Each paragraph must begin with a topic sentence.
• After you have read the topic sentence, write at least three more supporting sentences. Do not use bullets - use complete sentences.
• Make sure your paragraph is written with the specified pattern of organization.

"My Cousin's House"

Paragraphs 1 and 2

After many years of studying and working to put myself through the university, I finally graduated with a degree in architecture. Now I am licensed and am going to design luxurious mansions for wealthy clients who want "only the best."

My cousin, Tom Spencer, whom I haven't seen or heard from for at least ten years, contacted me and wants to be my first client. He has been living in an apartment and has just signed a contract with me to build an eight million dollar house for his wife, six year old triplets (1 girl and two boys), and him. Except for a few essential items, he has given me carte blanche. The essential items he wants are for me to find a beautiful setting on a large waterfront lot, a two story house, and a minimum of five bedrooms and five baths.

Write at least 3 more sentences which tell about all the "extras" you want for the house. Justify why you chose each "extra." The paragraph is started for you.

Paragraph 3: Use Topic List

As I sat at my drawing board, I started making a list of all the "extras" I think Tom would like for the house. He has been the only client I have ever had who has given me carte blanche. One idea I have is to build a

horse stable at the end of the property so the children could grow up with horses. Another…

_____

_____

_____

_____

_____

_____

_____

_____

You need to help finish the scheduling. Write at least three sentences which tell about five things a builder would need to do (in order) to complete a house from start to finish. (Although there are hundreds of "things", you only need to write about five.) Remember to explain why each one must be done before the next one. (For example, the walls are constructed before the roof is put on because the walls need to support the roof.)

Paragraph 4: Use Time-Order

_____

_____

_____

_____

_____

_____

_____

_____

Begin with a topic sentence and then write at least 3 sentences that give a visual description of the house. You may want to describe where the patio will be or the location and type of driveway. Use terms such as net to, near, beside, on top of, outside, in front of, around, next to, and surrounding.

Paragraph 5: Use Spatial

_____

_____

_____

_____

_____

_____

_____

_____

Write a topic sentence and with at least 3 more sentences to explain why Tom and his family are going live in the apartment.

Paragraph 6: Use Compare-Contrast

_____
_____
_____
_____
_____
_____
_____
_____

Write at least two more sentences to explain how the architect thinks Tom made millions of dollars to afford such a magnificent residence.

Paragraph 7: Use Caue-Effect
Tom, although you are my cousin, I never found out how you made all your money. I was so busy at school and, unfortunately, lost track of you.

_____
_____
_____
_____
_____
_____
_____
_____

What kind of home
would you design?

Write at least 2-3 sentences to define what Tom thinks a home should be.

Paragraph 8: Use Definition
I am very optimistic about the house. I feel confident that because this house is going to be so amazing, it will be featured in many magazines. But, Tom, every time you talk about the house, you refer to it as a home. Please give me your definition of a home.

_____
_____
_____
_____
_____
_____
_____

Chapter Summary

Authors usually develop their content information with a pattern of organization. Experienced readers who can recognize the pattern have an advantage over someone who can't detect the pattern. The advantage of using an organizational pattern is that it structures the information. This enables the reader to anticipate forthcoming information and thus increases comprehension.

Expository to Narrative Strategy

""If history were taught in the form of stories, it would never be forgotten."

Rudyard Kipling

Course: All courses

Goal: To remember information in a story (narrative format)

Material Needed: Textbook, paper, pencil, pen

Individual or group: Individual

Lesson Duration: 50-60 minutes

Finished Product to be graded: Make a copy of your "story."

Why do I need to learn this?

It's usually easier to remember a story than trying to remember textbook information. This strategy can turn a dull subject into an interesting and entertaining story that will be easy to remember.

Procedure

1. Choose a textbook reading assignment.

2. Read the selection.

3. Turn the selection into a story by saying something like, "Once upon a time, there_____" or another story starter.

4. An example of this strategy is given below. The several pages in a textbook that explains Jean Piaget's Formal Operation Stage were turned into a story.

An expository selection from a psychology textbook

According to Jean Piaget, there are four stages of development that children go through during their cognitive growth. They are the Sensori-motor, Preoperational, Concrete Operational, and Formal Operations. Formal Operations, the last and final stage, begins around age 12 and continues through adulthood. Piaget hypothesized that not every adult reaches Formal Operations. In fact, approximately only 35% of high school seniors reach Formal Operations by graduation and many people never reach this stage at all. The individual at the Formal Operations stage can demonstrate the ability to critically analyze situations, use logic, inference, and reasoning without manipulating concrete objects. He or she can think in abstract terms, can plan for the future, and arrive at multiple solutions to problems. He or she can also hold two pieces of information in mind and mentally manipulate them to solve problems. Have you noticed how some people can solve 2 and 3 step problems in their heads without using a paper and pencil? Another example is that someone in Formal Operations can solve problems such as, "Jim is taller than Mitch and shorter than Gene. Who is tallest?" Adolescents in Formal Operations solve abstract algebraic equations and visualize a two-dimensional drawing in three dimension. Some of these young people have a heightened self-consciousness and a sense of personal uniqueness. People in the Formal Operational stage like thinking in hypothetical possibilities, such as, "What would life be like if we had a cure for cancer?" and other abstract concepts such as justice, love, and inequality.

The following selection is a narrative that has been written based on the previous expository selection.

Mrs. Winkler, the 12th grade guidance counselor at Fall Springs High School in Fall Springs, Arkansas was ready to leave for the day when she got a call from her principal. "Please stay a little longer today because I have Jody Ingram in my office. She is very upset and is crying. I think you are the only one who can help her."

A few minutes later Jody came in, sat down and began telling me why she was so upset. She said all her friends became mean and started bullying her. They said she was a "goody-goody," always trying to be the "teacher's pet," always winning awards, having the highest GPA in the school, winning the chess tournament, and receiving a full scholarship to an Ivy League college. Her "friends" said she used to be "normal" but now she was so "different." They couldn't understand why she changed so much - why she wasn't more like them.

Mrs. Ingram thought for a few minutes and then asked her a few questions. She asked her to solve several 3-step problems in her head, change a 2 dimensional drawing to three dimensions, solve algebraic equations, and give two responses to the questions: "If everyone had the same religion, what would this world be like?" and "If you were to have one more eye, where would you place it?" When asked what she planned to do in the next ten years, Jody quickly replied that she planned to get a doctorate and have a career in research.

Mrs. Winkler said her friends were probably still in the Concrete Operations stage whereas Jody was definitely in the Formal Operations stage. Her friends are tied to immediate reality—they live in the "here and now" unlike Jody who lives in the world of possibilities. Mrs. Winkler explained Piaget's four stages of development and added that only 35% of high school students reach the Formal Operations stage. It appears that Jody's "friends" might never reach her level of mental development.

Jody felt so much better now that she understood why her friends were so mean and bulling her. She thanked Mrs. Winkler for her time and said she was glad graduation was a few weeks away. When she told Mrs. Winkler that as valedictorian, she had to give the commencement address. Mrs. Winkler then asked, "What will be the main theme of your speech?" Jody replied without hesitation, "What could our schools become without bullying?"

9
Understanding Visual/ Graphic Information

We remember 10% of what we hear, 20% of what we read, and 80% of what we see and interact with words.

Read this brief exchange between two high school seniors with perfect GPA's who are discussing results after the last exam. Read this because it may help you get an A on your next test.

Danny: "I can't believe I failed the history exam. I read every word in all three chapters. How could this happen? I'm not used to failing exams."

Abby: "That is such a shame. Did you study the charts, tables, and graphs like Mrs. Brown told us to do?"

Danny: "No, why study them when I read every chapter in detail? I think they're put in the book just to make it look good."

Abby: "That's why you failed, Danny. Don't you remember Mrs. Brown said to spend a lot of time on the charts, tables, and graphs? She said if you understand them and can explain them, you won't have to spend a lot of time reading the text. I did this and got an A."

Danny: "Wow! Oh, now I remember her telling us to do that. OK, I guess I'd better start paying attention to our teachers and all those graphs, tables, and charts."

Abby: "Right! And, I remember something else Mrs. Brown said that is really important. She said, "A picture is worth 1000 words.""

In this chapter you will read about:

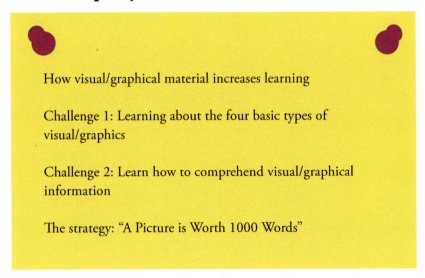

How visual/graphical material increases learning

Challenge 1: Learning about the four basic types of visual/graphics

Challenge 2: Learn how to comprehend visual/graphical information

The strategy: "A Picture is Worth 1000 Words"

Increase your learning: Use your textbook's visual/ graphic material

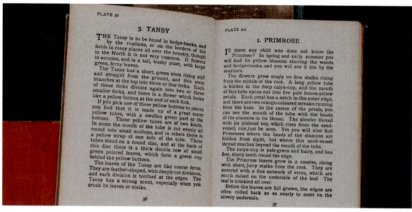

If your textbook has charges, graphs, tables, diagrams, and other visual material, consider yourself lucky. First of all, since it costs more to print information in visual form than it is to print words, sentences, and paragraphs, the author and publisher consider the visual information to be very important. Secondly, the visual/graphic material is not there for a decoration, it is there for instructional purposes.

You cannot pick up a textbook in any subject without finding a graphic aid, but many readers skip these aids completely in an effort to finish the reading faster. Writers use graphic aids to help the reader comprehend and remember the information. Writers know that some material is better expressed in graphical format rather than in written text, especially material that needs to be categorized.

70 – 75% of people respond better to visual information than to text.

Advantages of Visual/Graphical Aids

 Below are some reasons why visual/graphical material increases learning

 Graphs show relationships simply and easily.

Visual/graphical aids can summarize, explain complicated ideas, compare and contrast data, and present new and additional information. Sometimes a difficult concept is easier to comprehend with a visual/graphic aid rather than with words.

👉 Spending a minute or two looking at a chart, graph, map, illustration, and/or table before reading can simplify what you are expected to learn.

👉 Relationships between and among factors or variables displayed graphically/visually, in most cases, are easy to understand.

👉 Most of the time graphics can express with one chart, graph, table, or other visual several paragraphs or several pages of text.

👉 Studying visual graphic information impacts both sides of the brain.

👉 Studying graphic/visual material by covering up part of the graphic and recalling the information from memory is an efficient way to study for a test.

CHALLENGE 1
Learning about the four basic types of visual/graphics

Meeting the challenge: Complete Assignment 1-4

Bar Graph: Below is a sample and description of a Bar Graph.

A bar chart represents a series of values set horizontally or vertically according to the topics being studied. It is used to compare facts or quantities in different categories. The bar graph chart has rectangular lines or bars that vary in length. The bars go as high as the values it is representing.

Assessment 1:
Make a Bar Graph

College students, high school students, middle school students, elementary students and professionals all own many pairs of shoes. Professionals own 25 pairs each, college students own 15 pairs each, high school students own 10 pairs each, middle school students own 12 pairs each, and elementary students own 9 pairs each. Make a bar graph to show the different number of pairs of shoes. You may use the internet to help construct the bar graph. Be sure to label your graph.

Line Graph: Below is a sample and description of a Line Graph.

A line graph is a series of segmented lines or continuous curves that display data or information over time. The horizontal axis measures one feature and the vertical axis measures another variable which allows us to see the relationship and/or trends and increases and decreases between the two variables.

Assessment 2:
Make a Line Graph

The United States fought bravely in many wars. Memorial Day salutes the men and women who fought to keep this country free. Important dates and wars that are acknowledge on Memorial Day are:

War	Beginning Date	Date Ended
War of Independence	1775	1783
War of 1812	1812	1814
Mexican American War	1846	1848
American Civil War	1861	1865
World War I	1917	1918
World War II	1939	1945
Korean War	1950	1953
Vietnam War	1955	1975
Persian Gulf War	1990	1991
War on Terrorism	2001	present

Make Memorial Day graph of all the wars we fought. Use either the beginning dates or ending dates to make your chart. Write the names of the war on the horizontal line and the dates on the vertical line (Use increments of 25 years, e.g., 1775, 1880, 1825, 1850, etc.) You may consult the internet to give additional information. Give a title to the graph.

Pie Graph: Below is a sample and description of a Pie Graph.

A pie chart is circular representation of parts or percentages of the "total pie." In this chart, the circle is divided into sections or wedge-shaped slices giving a very clear image of the percentage of each section is in relation to the entire whole pie.

Assessment 3:
Make a Pie Graph

Preschool represents 10% of what is learned during a lifetime. Elementary school represents 15% of what is learned during a lifetime. Secondary school represents 20% and college represents 25% of what is learned in a lifetime. Life's experiences represent 30% of what is learned in a lifetime. Now, develop a pie chart that is segmented into these factors. Label each section and give the pie chart a name.

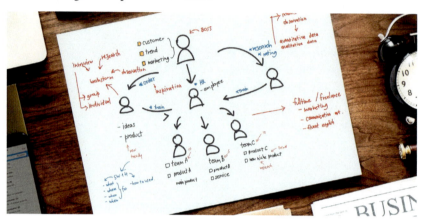

Flow Chart: Below is a sample and description of a Flow Chart.

Flow charts show the sequence or progression of events, procedures, or key ideas and the relationship between them. These ideas are presented in boxes and linked by arrows that allow the reader to see the progress or steps of the flow.

Assessment 4:
Make a Line Graph

Develop a flow chart for the following scenario below. Use a circle to describe the starting point and ending point. Use a rectangle to indicate steps. Use a triangle to indicate decisions that must be made along the way.

You have many friends coming to your dorm room on a Friday night. You decided to make a true Italian pizza for munchies. To start, you need to prepare the dough. You need to decide whether you should use white flour dough or whole meal flour dough. Make a decision. To prepare the dough you need flour, yeast, salt, water, and melted butter. You mix the dry ingredients together. Set them aside. Then you mix the wet ingredients. Set them aside. Next mix the dry and wet ingredients together. When you put them all together, set the dough aside. Next, slice mozzarella cheese, green peppers, onions, pepperoni, pineapple, and olives. Place these ingredients aside. You wonder if all of your guests would like olives and pineapple on the pizza. Make a decision if you want to use olives and pineapple on the pizza. Spread the dough on a pizza baking sheet. To the top of the dough, add a jar of pizza tomato sauce. Then add your ingredients one by one beginning with the cheese. Bake the pizza for 20 minutes in a 450 degree oven. Cut the pizza into slices while it is hot. Remember: Use a circle to describe the starting point and ending point. Use a rectangle to indicate steps. Use a triangle to indicate decisions that must be made along the way.

CHALLENGE 2
Learn how to comprehend visual/graphic information

We strongly recommend that you use the strategy, "Every Picture Tells a Story" because it is a general strategy that "works" for every visual/graphic in almost every course. To meet Challenge 2, apply "Every Picture Tells A Story" with a minimum of 4 visual/graphics from your textbooks. This strategy is easy to learn and we think it is very worthwhile especially when you realize how much you are learning!

Analyzing how correct and incorrect questions on graphic representation of items or groups are presented on a standardized test

Correct:
1. direct and exact response as represented by the graph and reading

Incorrect:
1. incorrect representation of the graph and reading

2. popular opinion of the items or groups but is not represented on the graph

3. very close representation of the items or groups on the graph

Chapter Summary

Some information can be presented more clearly visual/graphically than with words. It is important to understand the purpose and the main points. A visual/graphic can express in one diagram or chart what it might take words several pages to express the same thing.

 ## Every Picture Tells a Story

"A picture is worth 1000 words."

Course: All courses

Goal: To increase comprehension by using the visual/graphic material in the textbook

Material Needed: Textbook and other visual material for upcoming test, paper, pen, or pencil

Individual or group: Individual

Lesson Duration: Ongoing

Finished Product to be graded: Paper or notebooks that have main idea, purpose, and questions for each visual aid

Why do I need to learn this?

Students often overlook the visual/graphic material in their textbooks. This is a lost opportunity because visually displayed material presented is usually easier to understand than long, detailed paragraphs. Often one picture, chart, or graph can provide as much information as 2-3 paragraphs. "Every Picture Tells a Story" facilitates learning and understanding information in a concise, visual way.

Procedure

1. Select a chapter from a textbook.

2. Read the chapter's introduction to understand the main idea of the chapter.

3. Skim each page in the chapter to locate all the visual aids (graphs, charts, diagrams, maps, photos.)

4. Spend at least one to two minutes studying the visual aid, write the title of the visual aid on your paper, and read the caption.

5. Write the main idea, the purpose of the visual/graphic (e.g., the purpose of this visual is to show...) and write a minimum of 2-3 questions that a teacher might ask on a test.

6. Continue skimming each page of the chapter and repeat #5 for each visual aid.

7. Review the main idea, the purpose of the visual/graphic, and questions you wrote for each visual aid before reading the chapter in depth. Review several times more before a test.

Final Thoughts

There is a reason why maps, charts, graphs, illustrations, drawings, and other visual aids are found in textbooks. It is up to you, as a student, to discover the reason or purpose of each visual aid. Get into the habit of asking this simple question, "What am I supposed to learn from this visual aid? After awhile you will begin to realize that the 'age-old' idiom, "A Picture is Worth 1000 Words" is true!"

Many people, especially right-brained people and those strong in visual-spatial intelligence, find it easier to recall graphic material than to recall textual material. Another way to review would be to redraw the visual aid and then explain out-loud the purpose and the information it intended to convey.

Before reading the chapter, print all the main charts and graphs and write the main idea and purpose for each one. Notice that there is a link between each visual/graphic. Try to see the connection from the first visual/graphic to the succeeding ones. If you are able to understand the connection, reading the chapter will be much easier.

Final Thoughts

1.

It doesn't matter what kind of reader and writer you are now but it does matter what kind of reader and writer you will become, and

2.

More than ever the need to become proficient in reading and writing cannot be overemphasized.

Congratulations for completing Book 1: ***Become a Great Reader and Writer in College: Get the Basics Now.*** *You not have a firmer reading foundation and are ready for Book Two. The instruction and exercises in Book Two focus on the critical thinking in reading and writing skills you will need for the more challenging college courses in your future.*

Quotations
from Book One

"I keep seven honest serving men (they taught me all I knew); their names are What and Why and Where and When and How and Where and Who."

Rudyard Kipling

"Meaning is not in the words alone, but is largely in the reader."

Edmund B. Huey

"Don't tell me words don't matter. I have a dream. Just Words? We hold these truths to be self-evident, that all men are created equal. Just Words? We have nothing to fear but fear itself. Just Words?"

Barack Obama

"Colors face, temples crumble, empires fall but wise words endure."

Edward Thorndike

"How often misused words generate misleading thoughts."

Herbert Spencer

"Words are, of course, the most powerful drug of mankind."

Rudyard Kipling

"All the words I use in my stories can be found in the dictionary - it's just a matter of arranging them in the right sentences."

Somerset Maugham

"Reading usually precedes writing and the impulse to write is almost always fired by reading, the love of reading, is what you dream of - becoming a writer."

Susan Sontag

"The beginning of wisdom is calling things by their right name."

Confucius

"Trust yourself, you know more than you think you do."

Ben Franklin

"Effort matters more than intellect."

Author unknown

"Better three hours to soon than a minute too late."

William Shakespeare

"Between the pages of a book is a wonderful place to be."

Author unknown

Becoming A Great Reader and Writer In College

"Write, rewrite. When not writing or rewriting, read. I know of no shortcuts."
Larry. L. King

"The difference between something good and something great is attention to detail."
Charles R. Swindell

"It's the little details that are vital. Little things make big things happen."
John Wooden

"I learned no detail was too small. It was all about the details."
Brad Grey

"Success is the sum of details."
Harry S. Firestone

"As a journalist, the details always tell the story."
James McBride

"It's attention to detail that makes the difference between average and stunning."
Francis Atterbury

"When you pay attention to details, the big picture will take care of itself."
Georges St. Pierre

"Excellence is in the details. Give attention to details and excellence will come."
Perry Paxton

"When I was a little boy, they called me a liar; but now that I am a group-up, they call me a writer."
Isaac Bashevis Singer

"Between the pages of a book is a wonderful place to be."
Author unknown

"Writers don't have lifestyles. They sit in little rooms and write."
Norman Mailer

"Get it down. Take chances. It may be bad but it's the only way you can do anything really good."
William Faulkner

"If you only read the books everyone else is reading, you can only think what everyone else is thinking."

Haruki Murakami

"Anyone can be a writer but some writers convey thoughts and ideas better than others."

Joel Lopate

"The only writer to whom you should compare yourself is the writer you were yesterday."

David Schlosser

"Just write every day of your life. Read intensely. Then see what happens. Most of my friends who are put on that diet have very pleasant careers."

Ray Bradbury

"If history were taught in the form of stories, it would never be forgotten."

Rudyard Kipling

Index

Answer Key

Chapter 2: Challenge 2

<u>Exercise 1</u>

1.c, 2.b, 3.c, 4.b, 5.a 6.a 7.d, 8.b, 9.b, 10.b 11.b, 12.a, 13.c, 14.b, 15.d, 16.b, 17.a, 18.b, 19.d, 20.b

<u>Exercise 2</u>

1.c, 2.b, 3.c, 4.b, 5.a, 6.a, 7.d, 8.b, 9.b, 10.b, 11.b, 12.a, 13.c, 14.b, 15.d, 16.b, 17.a, 18.b, 19.d, 20.b

<u>Exercise 3</u>

1.foolish, senseless 2. agreeable, to be in accord 3.suspended in air, pause in flight 4.sensible judgment, wise 5. special language, idiom, 6. insignificant details, trivia 7. sheer, transparent 8. harmful, poisonous

<u>Exercise 4</u>

1.extrovert 2.Enthusiasm 3.unnoticed 4.casual and sloppy 5. lengthy 6.few 7.disorganized 8.suspicious

<u>Exercise 5</u>

1.similarity 2.intimation, hint 3.humor, jokes 4.ridicule, cutting remark 5.gloomy, sullen 6.rapidly recovering 7.uncontrollable 8.temporary

<u>Exercise 6</u>

1.a, 2.b, 3.c, 4.c, 5.a, 6.a, 7.c, 8.b, 9.b

<u>Exercise 7</u>

1.poverty, 2.beginner, 3.sorrowful, sad, 4.regretful, 5.wise, sensible, 6.principled, 7.reprimanded, 8.propensity, 9.double meaning, 10.misleading, 11.disagreement, 12.large store, 13.throaty, husky, 14.relieve, 15.astonished 16.handful, 17.recommend, 18.repetition, 19.conventional image, 20.taken back

<u>Exercise 8</u>

1.c, 2.b, 3.d, 4.a, 5.c, 6.b, 7.a, 8.d, 9.a, 10.c, 11.a, 12.a, 13.b, 14.d, 15.b, 16.a, 17.b, 18.d, 19.d, 20.a, 21.d, 22.c, 23.d, 24.a, 25.c, 26.b, 27.c, 28.b, 29.d, 30.a

<u>Exercise 9</u>

1.a, 2.c, 3.b, 4.Cc, 5.d, 6. b, 7.a, 8.a, 9.b, 10.a, 11.d, 12.b

Chapter 2: Challenge 3

Exercise 1

1.b, 2.b, 3.c, 4.a, 5.b, 6.d, 7.a, 8.c, 9.c, 10.a, 11.b, 12.a, 13.c, 14.d, 15.a, 16.a, 17.c, 18.b, 19.b, 20.a, 21.c, 22.d, 23.b, 24.d, 25.d, 26.a, 27.c, 28.b, 29.a, 30.b, 31.b, 32.a, 33.c, 34.a, 35.b, 36.b, 37.b, 38.c, 39.a, 40.c, 41.b, 42.b, 43.c, 44.c, 45.a, 46.b, 47.c, 48.b, 49.a, 50.c

Exercise 2

1.prefix, root, suffix 2. treasure 3. abridged, unabridged; abridged to class 4. production, reproducing, productivity 5. write dictionaries

Exercise 3: Answers will vary

Exercise 4

List 1: 1. F, 2. H,3. C, 4. I, 5. B, 6. G, 7. D, 8. E, 9. A, 10. J
List 2: 1. E, 2, I, 3. B, 4. F, 5. H, 6. A, 7. J, 8. D, 9. G, 10.C
List 3: 1. C, 2. G, 3. H, 4. I, 5. B, 6. D, 7.A, 8. F, 9. J, 10.E
List 4: 1. I, 2. F, 3. B, 4. J, 5. C, 6. E, 7. D, 8. A, 9. G, 10. H
List 5: 1. F, 2. I, 3, G, 4. A, 5. D, 6. B, 7. J, 8. E, 9. C, 10. H
List 6: 1. G, 2. A, 3. E, 4. H, 5. I, 6. B, 7. F, 8. C, 9. D, 10. J

Exercise 5

1. Hydrology, 2. Credible, 3. Respect, 4. Hydrophobia, 5.caption, 6. Contradict, 7. Perimeter, 8. Telegraph, 9. Hypodermic, 10. monarch, 12. Version, 12. Prediction, 13. Telephone, 14. Polygraph, 15. monograph, 16. Respectable, 17. Phonograph, 18. Diameter, 19. Chronology, 20. egoism, 21. Converse, convert, 22. Meteorology, 23. Demographic, 24. Subversion

Exercise 6

1.biceps, 2.Hypotension, 3.Contrast, 4.Reflection, 5.Automatic 6.combustion, 7.Comfortable, 8.Spectrum, 9.Collection, 10.Colony, 11.antibody, 12.Antibiotic, 13.Monotone, 14.Versatile, 15.Bilateral 16. democratic, 17.incredible, 18;.Biography, 19.Hydroplane, 20. Prescription, 21.geology, 22.Photography

Exercise 7

1.c, 2.b, 3.b, 4.c, 5.c, 6.a 7.b, 8.c, 9.b, 10.a, 11.d, 12.b, 13.b, 14.c, 15.a, 16. b, 17 .d, 18.a, 19.c., 20.c, 21.a, 22.b, 23.a, 24.c, 25.d, 26.a, 27.a, 28.b, 29.b, 30.b, 31.d, 32.a, 33.b, 34.c, 35.b, 36.b, 37.a, 38.c, 39.d, 40.b, 41.d, 42.d, 43.a, 44.c, 45.b, 46.a, 47.b, 48.d, 49.a, 50.c

Chapter 4
<u>Exercise 1</u>
1. First sentence, 2. First sentence, 3. First sentence, 4. last sentence
5. 4th sentence, 6. First sentence, 7. Last sentence, 8. Last sentence,
9. First sentence

<u>Exercise 2</u>
Exercises 1-10 answers will vary

<u>Exercise 3</u>
Exercises 1-8 answers will vary

Chapter 5
<u>Exercise1</u>
1-10 answers will vary

<u>Exercise 2</u> (answers may vary)
<u>1. Ray Charles</u>
Early Years
1.Born into poverty, 2.Became blind at 5 years, 3.Went to St. Augustine
School for Deaf and Blind, 4.Studied composition, 5.wrote music
in braille

Accomplishments
1.many accomplishments, 2.As famous as Billie Holliday and Elvis Presley

Hits
1.I Got a Woman, 2.What'd I Say, 3.Georgia on My Mind, 4.Hit the
Road, Jack , 5.Your Cheating Heart, 6.You Are My Sunshine

<u>2. Central Park</u>
History
1.Used to be a swamp, 2.Olmstead and Vaux architects, 3.Newcomers built
shanties, 4.First landscaped park, 5.1963 became historical landmark,
6. Greensward Plan took 15 years

Size and Statistics
1.843 acres, 2.Located in Manhattan, 3.Stretches 59th to 110 St. and from
5th to 8th ave.

Features of the Park
1.Lake, pond, 2.Zoo, 3.Skating rink, 4.English style garden, 5.Art shows,
6.concerts   7.Sporting events, 8.First landscaped park, 9.Most visited park
10.2.5 million visitors a year

3. Exam Stress
Preparing 3 weeks before finals
1.Assemble all notes, 2.Start textbook readings, 3.Handouts,
4.Get old tests, 5.Form a study

Preparing 1 week before finals
1.Predict test questions, 2.Use index cards for memorizing, 3.Reflect/think
about material, 4.What would professor want me to know?

4. Japan's Economy
Products Exported
1.Automobiles, 2.Electronics, 3.Computers, 4.Petrochemicals,
5.Pharmaceuticals, 6. Ships, 7.Aerospace products, 8.Textiles,
9.Processed food

Products Imported
1.Fuel, 2.Ore, 3.Metals, 4.Raw materials

Cultural Factors
1.Homogeneity of population, 2.High level of education, 3.Skilled labor,
4.Advanced technology, 5.Government provides incentives

5. White Collar Crimes
Definition
White collar criminals, Highly respected people, People of status,
People who commit crime for personal gain

Types of Crimes Committed
insider trading, bribery, forgery, embezzlement, computer crimes,
identity thefts

6. Designer Dogs
Why People Want Designer Dogs
1.Know how adult dog will look, 2. Easier to train, 3.Hypoallergenic,
4.Healthier, 5.Great companions, 6.Trendy, 7.unique and cute

Types of Designer Dogs
1.Labradoodles, 2.Goldendoodles, 3.cocapoos, 4.Peekapoos, 5.yorkipoos
6.Sheltipoos, 7.Maltipoos, 8.Shihpoos

7. Narcissistic Behavior
Facts about Narcissim
1.It's an epidemic, 2.Identify narcissism in a person before a relationship
gets serious

Traits of Narcissism
1.grandiose feelings, 3.Obsession with success/fame, etc., 3.Thinking they
are unique and special, 4.Need for excessive attention and adulation
5. Sense of entitlement, 6.Exploit others without guilt or remorse,
7.Devoid of sympathy, 8.Jealous of others

8. Edgar Allen Poe
Details of His Life
1.Orphaned at age 2, 2.Lived with foster family, 3.Miserable, lonely,
depressed during life, 4.Loved literature, read extensively, 5.began writing
poetry at UVA, 6.Father wanted Poe to get business degree, 7.Had a
tumultuous life - full of misery, 8.Died at age 41

Famous Works
1.The Raven, 2.The Black Cat, 3.The Tell-Tale Heart, 4.The Purloined Tale
5.Annabel Lee, 7.Eulalie, 8.The City and the Sea

Exercise 3
1-8 answers will vary

Exercise 4
1-5: Answers will vary.

6. Some Details about Popularity
1.Teens may suffer if not popular. 2.It is valuable for a ten to have a best
friend. 3.Being popular might be the most important thing in the world.

Subgroups of Popularity
1.Popular kids, 2.Amiable, 3.Neglected, 4.Rejected

Exercise 5
1.Her dress was made of rich materials, white satin, lace, and silk with a
white veil. 2.Her eyes were not bright and they were sunken. 3.The time
on her watch was twenty minutes to nine. 4. Miss Havisham touched
her heart. 5.They met in Miss Havisham's dressing room. 6.Pip had seen
waxwork figures at a fair. 7.Daylight 8.A veil and flowers. 9.They are
bright, sparkling jewels around her neck, on her hands, and on the table.
10.A mirror

Chapter 6 -7
Answers will vary

Chapter 8

<u>Exercise 1</u>
1.B, 2.C, 3.C, 4.A, 5.C, 6.A, 7.A, 8.A, 9.B, 10.c, 11.a, 12.b, 13.a, 14.b, 15.c

<u>Exercise 2</u>
1.Contrast, 2.Compare, 3.Topic-List, 4. Example/Illustrate, 5. Description
6.Definition, 7.Time-Order, 8.Cause-Effect, 9.Classification, 10.Summary

<u>Exercise 3</u>
1.A, 2.C, 3.C, 4.A, 5.B

<u>Exercise 4</u>
Answers will vary

Chapter 9
Answers will vary

Made in the USA
Columbia, SC
15 January 2020